Praise for *Cultivating Happiness*

'This is the moving, real-life story of a superheroine. And when such a story meets rigorous research in psychology and neuroscience, we have a book that instructs, elevates, and inspires.'

Dr Tal Ben-Shahar, Co-founder, Happiness Studies Academy, and internationally renowned teacher and author in the field of happiness and leadership

'How do you find happiness in the face of great loss? In the book *Cultivating Happiness*, Karen Guggenheim bravely shares her own personal story of pain and grief to illustrate the transformative power of post-traumatic growth, and provides tools and strategies to find happiness despite life's greatest challenges.'

Jen Fisher, Human Sustainability Lead at Deloitte US and bestselling author of *Work Better Together*

'Karen's commitment to happiness is incredible – her passion and dedication to both the science and concept of implementing happiness principles. Her approach is both inspirational and practical, and it has a direct connection to what I believe – that food is happiness, and moreover, its own language of happiness.'

Maria Loi, chef, entrepreneur, Greek food ambassador, philanthropist, author, TV host and lifestyle expert

'How can we proactively create the life we want, even when tragedy strikes? In this inspiring book, author Karen Guggenheim reveals happiness is teachable and learnable as she transforms a devastating personal loss into a global happiness movement. *Cultivating Happiness* takes us on an empowering journey beyond despair to find hope, happiness, and community using positive psychology principles as a roadmap. Reading this book feels like taking a life-changing road trip with a trusted friend who puts you back in the driver's seat of your life, past the pain, to destinations you never dreamed possible. Thank you, Karen, for this heartfelt gift to the world!'
Kelli Harding, MD, MPH, Psychiatrist and Public Health Physician, Columbia University Medical Center, author of *The Rabbit Effect: Live Longer, Happier and Healthier with the Groundbreaking Science of Kindness*

'*Cultivating Happiness* is a delightful science-based guide filled with practical tools and important information for those of us who want to enjoy a state of happiness, especially when life does not appear to be on our side.'
Sandro Formica, PhD, professor and speaker

'Karen's moving book provides such an inspirational real-world example of how you can learn from personal tragedy and channel your pain into a commitment to improve your happiness.'
Dr Laurie Santos, Chandrika and Ranjan Tandon Professor of Psychology, Yale University and host of *The Happiness Lab* podcast

'Loss, tragedy and trauma are among the toughest hurdles we face in our journey toward getting happier. In *Cultivating Happiness*, Karen Guggenheim charts a hopeful way forward for those who are suffering – complete with inspiring stories and insight into the best research. A must read.'

Dr Arthur C. Brooks, professor, Harvard Kennedy School and Harvard Business School, columnist at *The Atlantic* and #1 *New York Times* bestselling author

For Ricardo, Stefan and Kristof

Sonnet 18

Shall I compare thee to a summer's day?
Thou art more lovely and more temperate:
Rough winds do shake the darling buds of May,
And summer's lease hath all too short a date:
Sometime too hot the eye of heaven shines,
And often is his gold complexion dimmed;
And every fair from fair sometime declines,
By chance, or nature's changing course, untrimmed;
But thy eternal summer shall not fade,
Nor lose possession of that fair thou ow'st,
Nor shall death brag thou wander'st in his shade,
When in eternal lines to time thou grow'st.
So long as men can breathe, or eyes can see,
So long lives this, and this gives life to thee.

William Shakespeare, Sonnet 18

cultivating happiness

overcome trauma and positively transform your life

KAREN GUGGENHEIM

RIDER

1

Rider, an imprint of Ebury Publishing
20 Vauxhall Bridge Road
London SW1V 2SA

Rider is part of the Penguin Random House group of companies
whose addresses can be found at global.penguinrandomhouse.com

First published as *Coltiva La Tua Felicità* by Rizzoli in 2023
This edition published in Great Britain by Rider in 2024

www.penguin.co.uk

A CIP catalogue record for this book is available from the British Library

ISBN 9781846047800

Typeset in 12.5/17pt Baskerville MT Pro by Jouve (UK), Milton Keynes
Printed and bound in Great Britain by Clays Ltd, Elcograf S.p.A.

The authorised representative in the EEA is Penguin Random House Ireland,
Morrison Chambers, 32 Nassau Street, Dublin D02 YH68

Penguin Random House is committed to a sustainable future
for our business, our readers and our planet. This book is made
from Forest Stewardship Council® certified paper.

CONTENTS

PART 4: RELATIONSHIPS

PART 5: ENHANCED SPIRITUALITY

FOREWORD BY MO GAWDAT

It was a partnership at first sight. I was just about to release my first book, *Solve for Happy*, when a friend of mine at Google suggested that I speak to Karen. He said she was about to launch an event, the World Happiness Summit (WOHASU), around the same time as the publication day of the book with the intention of spreading a message of happiness. He said we seemed like a perfect match and offered to introduce us.

With less than three weeks to go before the summit and the publication of my book, I didn't think much would come out of a call with Karen. Yet, believing in serendipity, I decided to take the call anyway.

There she was, in the midst of the rush that precedes an event of that scale. Everything about her was radiating excitement. So much energy, so many ideas and such high expectations of what was about to become. She said, 'The world needs this, Mo. Our world deserves to be happy.'

Despite the screen of a video conference separating us, I couldn't help but feel her energy and commitment. Whenever you're in Karen's presence you feel that positivity.

I asked her, 'Why are you putting so much effort and resources into this?' Her answer was the perfect match for why I was doing what *I* was doing.

Three years earlier, I had lost my wonderful son, Ali, to a preventable medical error. My response to that tragedy was to write a book about happiness, a book that would teach the world what he had taught me. It was my way of keeping his memory alive and telling the world that happiness is attainable, even in the harshest of circumstances. Asking Karen why she was launching WOHASU, she said it was to keep the memory of her late husband, Ricardo, alive and to spread happiness to the world the way he showed her how to be happy.

There you go. Perfect Match. Instant partners.

Three weeks later I showed up in Miami to an event that was painted with Karen's values and true colours. Volunteers who happily gave all they could to help, speakers from all walks of life and corners of the globe who shared knowledge and experience and even the attendees had that selflessness to them. They were not there just to be happy but to make others happy, too. Karen rushed around. She never had a moment to relax. Driven by a desire to make WOHASU a once-in-a-lifetime experience for all who came.

Coming from my long-standing corporate career where I only attended events that discussed tech, business and money, I remember that my first impression of WOHASU was that I had never been hugged so much in one day in my whole life. There was such a beautiful vibe in the air. Karen had managed to bring together like-minded, like-hearted people who truly cared about making a difference, not only to themselves, but to everyone around them.

One hug in particular, though, was the most memorable. That was when I saw Karen herself for the first time. Instant friends. No – perhaps old friends who have been there for each other, life after life. Years later, still today, we've always popped up in each other's lives in ways that were not only supportive but always, always joyful, too.

Since that day, I have spoken at every single WOHASU. Not for the hugs, though those are truly a plus. But for the genuine intention that Karen infuses into what she does, that intention that is uniquely Karen.

The happiness business, if it is correct to call it such, is filled with coaches, gurus, therapists, yogis, teachers, healers, authors, chief happiness officers, as well as big pharma itself. Everyone claims they have found the magic bullet, and everyone seeks attention and recognition. Some do it for the money, some for ego and some to find their own path to happiness. Some see it as a job, while others a passion. Some are good at it, while others need a bit more time.

Of all of those, I've only ever met a few who do what they do because they genuinely want to make a difference above all else. Of those, Karen, with her commitment, dedication, vulnerability, endless energy and positivity, is a precious gem. She'll give herself for the happiness of her audience and she truly practises what she preaches. Her story of building WOHASU is a testimony to what is possible when someone chooses to make a difference and follows through with effort and dedication.

I've been waiting for Karen's first book for a while because I think this story will inspire so many to follow suit and make happiness – not only for themselves, but also for others – their top priority, then actually deliver on the promise. I hope you will be one of those. I hope you will enjoy every page of this book as much as I did, and I hope that while you read, you will send Karen positive vibes to keep her going on her quest to make our world a better place.

Mo Gawdat, January 2023

INTRODUCTION

Most of us have heard of post-traumatic stress disorder or PTSD, but I had never heard of post-traumatic growth (PTG). It's interesting that we are very up to date with all that can go wrong and doesn't work in life, but somewhat oblivious to what does – and can – go right. It seems that some people can grow after adversity and trauma. And it turns out that I am one of them.

I was clueless that PTG existed and even more so that I had actually experienced it. It was only after a conversation with mindfulness professor Dr Itai Ivtzan, while planning the World Happiness Summit, that I realised that not only had I gone through it, but I may have had expertise in it myself. I will share how I became capable of experiencing great happiness and fulfilment after sudden tragedy, loss and trauma. Sadly, because of the COVID-19 epidemic, millions of people around the world have recently experienced losing a loved one and may be struggling as a consequence.

I lived a similar experience. But through purpose and meaning, I was able to discover that happiness is teachable and learnable; through action, I was able to understand the importance of repetition and reframing for sustainable wellbeing and happiness; and through service, I was able to foster a global movement centred on positivity, compassion and kindness.

This book is based on my experiences as a social entrepreneur leading WOHASU, the wellbeing platform named after the World Happiness Summit, the leading happiness conference in the world. Along with an amazing team and community, I am honoured to organise the summit and provide experts with a vehicle through which to share research-based tools for positive change with a global audience.

There is a relatively new science behind my healing and transformation, but I didn't know it at the time. My first degrees were in *traditional* psychology and journalism. But it was not until 1998 that Dr Martin Seligman made his famous address as president of the American Psychological Association, in which he challenged researchers and psychologists to study the results of flourishing minds that forever changed psychology. So positive psychology was not yet a choice of study for me when I was in college.

My goal now is to expand the learning that I have acquired from the work of leading social thinkers and practitioners who dedicated their lives to researching wellbeing, happiness and positive psychology, and show how we can benefit from this science.

Pioneer doctors Richard G. Tedeschi and Lawrence G. Calhoun define post-traumatic growth as the 'positive psychological changes experienced as a result of the struggle'. Interestingly, several events that happened in my childhood allowed me to become resilient, making growth post trauma more accessible. I was born in Nicaragua, one of the poorest countries in the western hemisphere, and saw much poverty and unfairness. I believe witnessing this as a child increased my capacity for empathy. I left my country when I was nine years old because of the civil war that pitted families and friends against each other. I experienced the shock of leaving my life in Nicaragua and moving to the United States, and attended school in English without knowing the language. Plus, I am dyslexic. I struggled, fought and persevered, graduating with top honours and receiving scholarships to universities. Living through these events and learning from them helped me to develop the resiliency muscle that would later set my life on a new course.

While I have strong resiliency skills, what I experienced after losing my husband was beyond resilience. Because I did not bounce back to my set point – I surpassed it. The experience was so shockingly painful, tragic and defining. My life shattered. Yet I was able to undergo transformational growth, even creating a company focused on increasing global happiness and wellbeing and developing the World Happiness Summit. Growing from my husband's death led me to become a leader in the global happiness movement. It sounds strange, even when I write it now. To understand the growth, you must understand the loss. My husband was magnificent. While my story has sadness, it is really a legacy of hope and love.

I have divided this book into five main areas where I experienced positive change, as defined by Tedeschi and Calhoun in the Post-Traumatic Growth Inventory:

I. New possibilities in life: it's a choice – develop new paths and habits, innovation and adaptation.

II. Greater personal strength: discover undiscovered inner capacities and strength.

III. New appreciation of life: notice the value of life, feel appreciative and grateful.

IV. Relationships: new deeper connections, especially to those who have experienced pain.

V. Enhanced spirituality: connect or reconnect with core beliefs.

In each chapter, I tell how different principles and expert research and frameworks supported my transformation.

And at the end of each one, I offer some tips that helped me and other options which were not beneficial to me but may work for you or your loved ones.

One of the things I love about happiness is that it's subjective. It is level ground for conversation and discussion because no two people achieve and sustain happiness in exactly the same way. It is like discussing a favourite colour. There is no right or wrong. It is universal that happiness feels good, and its pursuit should not harm others. We are actually hardwired to feel better by helping people. To do otherwise is to work against nature. Not a good idea, but that is a subject for another time.

I share my story because I want to ignite a vision that it is possible to experience growth after loss and trauma, cultivate happiness and rewrite your narrative to live a satisfying, hopeful and happier life – and one that acknowledges grieving as a natural part of it. If you are fortunate enough not to have gone through really challenging times, then please use this story and knowledge to become happier and help others who might not be as fortunate. There is no downside to advocating for wellbeing; individuals do better physically, mentally and emotionally, we have better relationships, kids perform better in school, we are more engaged and productive at work, and communities where the focus is equity, fairness and inclusion thrive more than those that don't invest in fostering these wellbeing principles. I've used evidence-based practical tools that are learnable and, when used over time, these can effect positive change, offering a framework for hope. I am grateful to all the amazing experts for their work and generosity in bringing this knowledge to the world.

My journey is based on reality and begins with loss. Because guess what? Painful things are painful.

PART 1

NEW POSSIBILITIES IN LIFE

1

TRAUMA – PAIN AND LOSS AS CATALYSTS FOR CHANGE

'Pain can change you, but that doesn't mean it has to be a bad change. Take that pain and turn it into wisdom.'

Dalai Lama

A few days before the first World Happiness Summit (WOHASU) in March 2017, I was being interviewed live on an international primetime news talk show and was asked if attending WOHASU would stop people from feeling sadness. As happiness expert Dr Tal Ben-Shahar says, 'There are only two kinds of people who don't feel negative emotions: psychopaths and dead people'. The good news is that if you do feel negative emotions, it means you are not a psychopath and you are alive.

There is no magic pill or 'five tips to happiness' that will inoculate you from experiencing the full range of human emotions – because all of us are, well, human. Happiness is a process. It is remarkable that we are constantly trying to fight against our natures, run away from how our brains function and tend to be generally unaware of our biology, especially about how our thoughts and emotions impact our wellbeing or lack thereof. Yet, we should not be too self-critical; after all, we learned just about everything in school, except about ourselves.

Most importantly, very few people were taught that, while we may not have control over things that can happen in our lives, we do have a choice in how we react to them. So why do we react the way that we do? What are the ways of being that help us become healthier and happier? What are the stories we tell ourselves about ourselves? How do we create limiting beliefs? What are the biological and professional benefits of happiness?

I used to think that happiness was outside myself. I was happy if my husband was home more often, if I travelled to a new city, if my kids excelled, if I received compliments, if I got a good parking spot at the mall. I had never connected with the direct impact or influence I had on my own happiness and feeling of wellbeing. So I did not realise that I could make decisions that could help me feel happier and well. My life was like a boat on the ocean, moved left or right by the waves, riding the current, rudderless, with nobody steering, least of all me.

It was not until I lost my husband, mentor and love of my life that I learned that I had a say in my happiness. So many of my needs were tied up in this one person and I was profoundly torn when he died. He caught the flu, and, within ten days, his physical presence was gone. I cannot say he was gone altogether because he is so very present in our two children, in the memories of his friends and family and in my heart. He is alive to me because I choose to focus on the part that he lived. Yes, he died, but he also lived, and his impact was felt by many. It is not possible to erase his memory. Ricardo was an intricate combination of excellence, compassion, elegance, mystique, hard work and, above all, kindness. That was my husband, a complex genius.

My best friend and partner of twenty-one years died, and I wanted to die, too. Not because of a morbid sense or depression, but because I felt like I was done with life. I felt like I had finished a magnificent multi-course meal in a beautiful restaurant, and was offered dessert, but I wanted to ask for the bill so that I could go home because I was satisfied. One more thing would have spoiled the meal.

He was the best person I ever met. He was unbound generosity, wit and charm. It was a privilege to be in the presence of his brilliance, to see how his brain worked. He was a neurosurgeon at twenty-four years old, went on to also become an anaesthetist at a level-1 trauma centre and earned an MBA from the University of Chicago. Yet he was never conceited or pompous, but humble and kind. In a world where you can be anything, and Ricardo was many things, he chose to be kind. He overcame much emotional anguish and a bone-marrow transplant. He was resilient and never a victim. His legacy of kindness lives on in my work.

Simply, after he died, my concept of my life was gone, and I was finished. When he died, I experienced the much-described 'fork-in-the-road' moment. I saw life and death and was courted by desires of the latter. Then, I heard a voice, a soft whisper asking me, 'What about the children?' Oh no. My two beautiful boys, just starting their lives, searching for their wings. Even though they'd experienced their father's cancer scare, they had lived in blissful ignorance of how utterly unfair and hard life can be sometimes.

I knew that I had to live because of my love for them and because they needed me. It was so difficult to decide to live, so appealing to just let go and bypass the pain. But there was not going to be an easy way out. So I decided to live. And having done so, I immediately decided that I would have to live happily. I didn't know how to do that and certainly didn't feel it, but I knew that I couldn't live with myself as a victim; one, because I couldn't stand being pitied, and two, because I would be useless to my children. And what would be the point of being here in that case?

That's why I have devoted a whole chapter to the narratives we create that make the blueprints for our lives. I refused the victim narrative in my life. I would not be labelled the 'young widow' wherever I went. I hate that word. Just five letters, but they pack a punch. There are many stories attached to words; often, we are not even aware of them. When I thought of the word 'widow', I thought back to all the movies I had seen where beautiful, vibrant women ended up with an infinite wardrobe of black dresses, lifeless faces – many of them consigned to living as nuns or in seclusion. The death of one meaning the end of two lives.

Even though I became a widow at just forty-two years old, that label would not define me and I would not live that story. I am not what happened to me. I am who I choose to be. I chose happiness before feeling happy; I decided to become the hero of my own story. I had to write a new narrative. And death would not be the end; it would be the beginning. In fact, I only wore black once, for the funeral, and I threw away the dress when I got home. My hurt is carried inside, deep; adding further sadness to it will not bring him back and just fuels the pain.

One Christmas (before Ricardo died), my nephew had given me a T-shirt that said: 'I am Happiness'. I thought, we wear shirts for the sports teams that we support, why not wear a shirt to support what I wanted in my life, what I eventually wanted to be. The choice to become happy provided a beacon, much like a lighthouse guides a boat through treacherous waters at night. So, I put the shirt on. I tried different things and repeated the ones that worked for me, eventually learning that there is scientific evidence for why this works.

For me, the bridge to happiness was through purpose and meaning. I decided to focus on what I could control out of an uncontrollable event. I found that I could try to create something good out of something bad. Growing up, my dream was to attend Georgetown University in Washington, DC. I didn't go because I got married. Four months after Ricardo died, I decided that I would go to Georgetown School of Business for my MBA as a 'gift' to my husband – a remembrance and homage to his memory.

I knew that he would be so proud, and that gave me solace and comfort. It gave me meaning that served as an anchor when I felt I was drowning. It was a beacon in my darkness. A new story was being written, and I was writing it. This gave me a sense of agency, which is vital to wellbeing. It is important to note that no trauma or loss is trivial. What matters is the significance of the event for the person. And the tools and methods for recovery and growth will build resilience and can be used by all.

I started making new social connections at university, creating new friendships and feeling a sense of belonging, which made me feel happier. I learned new things, like business analytics, accounting and finance. Learning something new is a fantastic way to foster wellbeing. So I combined purpose, learning something new and cultivating relationships, which are all research-based methods to become happier.

Every day, I started with music in the morning while getting ready for the day, something I still do today. And, if possible, I dance. Movement, as I will discuss more later (see page 57), is incredibly important to humans, especially when we are down. I don't wait to be happy to listen to music; I play the songs as part of my daily ritual to prime my mind for feeling good, optimistic and hopeful, even when I am feeling sad or anxious. Positive habits are crucial for us to develop ways of being that support sustainable wellbeing.

I used my imagination and started to think that maybe my life could make sense again and that my children would thrive. Picturing a future in which laughter could be heard, and new stories could be written became my driving force.

We often catastrophise about our lives and futures, even when nothing harmful is going on. Many of us tend to think about negative things happening in the future and we are afraid to think of wonderful ones because either we might be disappointed or we might bring bad luck. But this is nonsense, and in so doing, we only squander our todays in fear of events that never arrive. What a waste. Instead, I started to look at the future as being filled with new opportunities. What if things turned out right? What if things went well? I also started to stay present and began practising mindfulness without really being aware that I was doing it. I noticed that if I stayed in the now, I wasn't afraid and sad. Yoga helped me, too, as did studying challenging subjects.

Then, a year into my journey, I experienced a setback. On the eve of the one-year anniversary of Ricardo's death – and, by the way, he died on my only sister's birthday, making 6 March a bittersweet day of celebration and remembrance – I thought, Now, after one year it won't hurt any more. Well, I was very wrong. I believed that if I just made it through the first year, celebrating all family occasions without him, then I will have 'made it' out of the suffering. It doesn't work like that, though. There are no exact steps in grieving and no two people grieve the same way. On the day of the anniversary, I realised that this was going to hurt for ever – in different ways, at different times and with different intensities. This realisation brought me much sadness. Yet I accepted it, since I was committed to making meaning out of the event and reinventing myself and my life. There *would* be a new story.

The way forward was one foot after the other, walking into the unknown. These steps, and others that I took towards constructing happiness, I later learned are evidence-based tools to foster wellbeing. According to happiness researcher Dr Sonja Lyubomirsky, 'Happy people are inclined to perceive and interpret their environment differently from their less happy peers'. Dr Lyubomirsky's work shows us that how people think, how they are motivated and how they act demonstrates why some are happier than others. These processes have a greater impact on our happiness than our life circumstances.

Much of my journey was an intuitive, yet haphazard approach to becoming happier. The shock and trauma of the sudden loss pushed me into action. I became very motivated to make meaning out of the event and move towards my goal. Discovering the science of happiness helped me not only to cope with the loss, but also to grow from the experience. When I understood that happiness was learnable and teachable, I decided to dedicate my life to creating a platform to bring this new science to a global audience. I chose to create a legacy of hope through the World Happiness Summit.

TIPS

1. For one week, keep a journal of three things that went well each day and describe how you felt, where you were and how they happened. Be as descriptive as possible.

2. Search for jokes. Use humour to 'hack' repetitive negative thoughts and give you a mood boost through laughter. It is a powerful feel-good tool because of the endorphins it releases, and it is also a great enhancer of social connection.

3. Think of one goal you would like to achieve. You can start small. Notice successes along the path and celebrate them. Become aware of how you feel when you go one step forward towards your goal.

2

NEUROPLASTICITY – HOW I REWIRED MY BRAIN

'Picture your brain forming new connections as you meet the challenge and learn. Keep on going.'

Carol Dweck, American psychologist

Two years after my life broke after suddenly losing my husband, I became aware that I had instinctively used tools that science had found to positively affect our lives and increase happiness. I don't know where this intuition came from, but I was surprised at how I had *accidentally* become happy again. In fact, I have experienced moments of great joy, satisfaction, purpose and flow during the time that I was growing through pain.

What is happiness? (It's important to note that when

I use the term 'happiness', I am referring to the academic sense of happiness or subjective wellbeing, typically defined by researchers as 'people's cognitive and affective evaluations of their lives'.) Happiness is more than pleasure. From a conversation with happiness researcher and positive-psychology coaching expert Dr Robert Biswas-Diener, I gathered that happiness is a subjective experience felt inside by each individual and comprises different components. Humans are not made to be 'happy' all the time, but we can work on many things that give our lives meaning and satisfaction. This is what *I* did. I focused and worked hard on developing positive relationships, mindfulness, life purpose and a deeper sense of community; I invested in choices that created more meaning in my life.

Individuals have a general sense that life is going well, and it is universal that happiness feels good. It has two components: emotional and cognitive. We understand the emotional part – this is the part that feels good. The cognitive, or *thinking* part is tied to engagement, relationships, meaning and accomplishment. And this is the part that I believe is most important for the sustainability of positive emotions – because it is the part that we have control over. The wonderful thing is that as I invested in these elements, those around me also became happier; my children, friends and family all benefitted from the ripple effect that happiness can have. It is, in fact, contagious. As I healed myself, my kids healed, too, and thrived. Of course, they experienced the pain and low moments – there is no way around all of that – but they also saw a new vision of what life could be.

When you are struggling with feeling happy, focus on friendships, call someone to offer help, learn a new language or simply move your body. Don't wait until you want to do it – just do it and see how you feel after. Perhaps you might not immediately feel happier, but over time, through trial and error, you can find what works for you.

If you want to be happier, invest in activities that put you in a flow state – a state of effortless attention, where you are completely immersed in what you are doing, losing all sense of time when you are engaged in them. Create, foster and nurture healthy social connections, deepen your relationships. Question what your life purpose is. What are you passionate about? How can you contribute to making something better? Find purpose in your life, including what you can do for others. And put your energies into areas that will fill you with a sense of accomplishment to develop a growth mindset (a way of thinking that encourages us to view challenges and setbacks as opportunities for learning).

In looking at happiness in this way, we can see that it encompasses the whole range of human emotions, not just positive ones; embracing all feelings is an important step towards sustainable happiness and overall health and wellbeing. Through the various benefits associated with feeling happier and well, we see that paying attention to it is very important during 'good' times, but even more so in 'challenging' times. It is actually a competitive advantage and significant to our survival – because research shows that happier people live longer, have better immune systems, recover faster from illness and have increased wellbeing, meaning that they are more optimistic, have less cardiovascular disease and are more resilient.

The first step to growing from trauma was changing my mind to look for the positive, so that I could create significance out of what had happened. Immediately after the loss, I was in a state of shock for about four months. The colours of the world around me looked different. The sounds I heard were muffled, like when you are underwater, and you hear people speaking but you cannot understand what they are saying. I could not make sense of what had happened – or of life itself. I couldn't really believe it. I had to make myself understand and then accept that he was gone, that the way my family had been structured was finished and the future would be completely different. I had to lean into the unknown and it was very scary. It still is sometimes. For many years, I had flashbacks of the emergency room where he died, with the team of doctors and nurses trying to save him. I got through that experience in the ER by focusing on my breath, through prayer and gratitude for having had such an amazing person as the father of my children. This took effort on my part; I chose not to feel sorry for myself.

Things happen in life because they just happen. And this was one of those events. I had to look at life in a different way, so I decided to do just that. It was clear to me that I had to change inside before I could change my circumstances. While I was still heartbroken, I chose happiness because I knew that if I would choose to be just *ok,* I would not make it. I had to shoot for the stars, for what seemed at the time out of reach. This gave me the hope I needed.

Our brains are like filing cabinets for experiences. We experience what we notice. We cannot attend to everything going on around us – there are too many stimuli – so we 'filter' our reality. If we have ingrained negative thought patterns, then we will fill those cabinets with experiences that match up. Sometimes we have blind spots for the good that is happening in our lives. We need to purposely look for it, so that we create new frames through which to look at the totality of our experiences, not only what we have conditioned ourselves to perceive from a lifetime of experiences. But why do we tend to remember the bad and struggle to remember the good? The negative sticks generally five times as much as the positive; additionally, research has found that when making decisions, people tend to give more weight to the negative components of an experience than positive ones. And we have evolution to thank for that one. Our brains are naturally wired to scope out danger, so that we can act and survive. In fact, we have been in survival mode since the sabre-toothed tiger was lurking behind a rock, ready to catch us. Looking out for the negative was very useful from an evolutionary perspective because it helped to keep us safe. But the consequence of being in fight-or-flight mode (an automatic physiological reaction to an event that is perceived as stressful or frightening) is a continuous flow of cortisol in our bodies, which can make us ill over time. When danger is there, this is both called for and effective in securing our safety, but when we react that way at work, at home or in traffic, it can be not only counterproductive, but also dangerous, causing responses that are out of sync with reality. So our innate negativity bias means that many of us have wired our brains, through repeated thoughts and actions, in ways that are not really that helpful and not primed for happiness.

There is a widely held misconception that to be happy we should negate the challenges of life or sugarcoat what is really going on. But a true understanding of happiness is a choice to *see* both the good and the bad, but to focus on the good. Experts say that when you appreciate the good, the good appreciates. I was not a happy person by nature. In fact, I was pretty pessimistic because I mostly focused on the negative side of things and paid little attention to what was going right in my life. I took all that for granted. I evolved through the purposeful selection of looking for what was good in my life, the good in others and new opportunities – not just focusing on the bad. I chose to focus on the fact that my husband had lived, and I tapped into the courage inside me which told me that I would be all right. And by me being 'ok', so would my children. I reframed.

We use frames to understand perceptions. Because of the neuroplasticity of the brain, we can change our frames or mindsets. We can rewire our brains in positive and productive ways. When I realised this, my life changed. Or better said: I changed my life, but it did have to start with changing me. The way I saw it before my new awareness, it was as if I was sitting on a bench waiting for the happiness bus to arrive and for me to get on it. Happiness, I thought, would come externally. I had a perception that this happiness was a certain way and not within my control, but when life rocked my world – when I fell off the bench – I realised that I had to change my perception. I became aware that the bus could be different colours and that sometimes I had to make an effort and walk to it. As I changed my mind, my life started to change, too. It began with awareness, a paradigm shift, choice and action. This is the entire way to happiness in a nutshell.

An amazing point about our wiring is that many of the things we do are on loops. Negative behaviours and thoughts can produce unwanted and detrimental outcomes that result in declining mental and physical health and happiness. I remember ruminating about things that didn't turn out how I wanted, or thinking over and over again about something that someone had said or done that hurt me or that I didn't like. I also used to take things personally, even when something did not have to do with me. I would also think about events that I was afraid would happen and rehearse conversations in my head that would never take place. What a waste of energy and time. Most of the things that we worry about never happen, but by engaging in these loops, we experience them as if they have occurred.

But the opposite is true, too. Behaviours that prime our brain towards the positive also create loops. Scanning for the good by engaging in gratitude, acknowledging people for an accomplishment or carrying out random acts of kindness makes us feel better – and happier people are kinder, more altruistic, thereby creating a ripple effect of positivity for the self and others. In initiating more opportunities for win-win scenarios, we invest in and move the needle towards the kinds of relationships, organisations, communities and societies that we want to create.

I started thinking about what would happen if things went well. What would that look like? I used visualisation and imagination to create an optimistic future. What if I excelled in my business programme or became a social entrepreneur? What if I lost my fear of public speaking and became an inspirational speaker? What if I fostered a happiness movement birthed from unhappiness?

It would be great if someone else could make us happy, or if something we bought, a promotion or a new house would do it. Maybe our children's accomplishments? But while these will likely give us joy in the moment, this is only temporary – and it's all because of biology again.

We have something called an adaptability bias. We humans are programmed to survive, so we can adapt to almost any circumstance; this is called hedonic adaptation. In fact, research shows that people who win the lottery will revert to their happiness set point after some time. The shiny, new things or experiences that give us momentary joy do not produce sustainable happiness. The only way to sustainable happiness is working on the self; it is an ongoing inside job. And the beauty of how this works is that truly happy people are also empathetic and altruistic. According to Dr Martin Seligman, altruism is one of the best routes for meaningful life satisfaction: 'We are wired to feel well through altruism'.

The way I have come to understand it is that happiness is a process – a by-product of purposely living a meaningful life, accomplished through engaging in actions that, over time, become habits, rewiring our naturally 'negative' brains to elevate wellbeing and increase more opportunities for positive emotions. It is fascinating that we can really 'feel the science' by engaging in these evidence-based behaviours.

Happiness expert Tal Ben-Shahar, who taught two of the most popular classes in the history of Harvard, talks about how the pursuit of happiness is both selfish *and* selfless. It benefits the self but, at the same time, the process of becoming happier ripples out to others around you. It's been said that you can keep sadness inside, out of sight, but that happiness cannot be hidden. It bursts out and is contagious. The happier I became, the more I wanted to share it, and in organising the World Happiness Summit, I get to spread the science and tell people about my growth experience and happiness journey. Which, consequently, makes me feel happier and more fulfilled, with an increased sense of optimism, hope and gratitude. This loop mechanism is expansive and allows me to feel happier still.

It turns out that the same emotional channel through which we feel happiness is where we feel loss, too. Big loss and pain can expand the capacity of the channel, and if you can fight through the pain, there are rewards on the other side. My capacity to love and care for others, my desire to pursue new ventures, my excitement for life and my compassion were all multiplied exponentially after losing my husband. It was unexpected. This book tells you how it works.

TIPS

1. How do you define happiness? Which aspect of your happiness do you think you can develop? Write down three reasons why these matter to you.

2. How does your body feel when you are in fight-or-flight mode? Use this information to alert you to something that you need to pay attention to.

3. To learn the 'art' of reframing, watch your favourite movie and try to find the good in the most difficult scenarios. Then begin using the same strategy in your life.

3

LEARNING SOMETHING NEW AND CONNECTING WITH PURPOSE

'I learned that courage was not the absence of fear, but the triumph over it. The brave man is not he who does not feel afraid, but he who conquers that fear.'

Nelson Mandela

When I was growing up, my dream was to go to Georgetown, Washington, DC. Having been born in Nicaragua to a multicultural, international family who often discussed history and politics, I was interested in studying foreign relations, and attending Georgetown was my goal. I applied after high school; I was waitlisted and didn't get in. A year and a half later, I reapplied and was admitted as a transfer student.

Ricardo, my then boyfriend and eleven years my senior, said that he would go with me and find a position as an anaesthetist there. He asked me to marry him and at just twenty-one years old, I said yes to him, and no to Georgetown. I didn't think that I could be a wife and a student at an elite university; I thought it was an either-or situation. I don't even know why I believed that. It was just there, like a certainty, even though I had no reason or life experience to base it on. This, as I now know, is an example of a limiting belief. We are deeply impacted by the cultures and families we are born into and develop ways of thinking that become naturally aligned to their norms. We are largely not aware that we even have them and, as a result, it is difficult to change as adults. They are embedded in us and feel natural, just like breathing.

Limiting beliefs place us in scarcity mindsets, which narrow our opportunities because we believe (often wrongly) our thoughts to be absolute truths, and this can stop us from taking certain actions. Significantly, humans have around 50,000 thoughts a day and most are negative because of our negative bias. Imagine how much that can skew our outlook.

To have a true representation of reality, we need to also look at what is going *right* in our lives. This is where mindfulness is especially helpful. If we take care to ground ourselves in the now, and not mind travel to the future and the past, we are able to realise that largely, we are ok. We can also make better decisions that are not clouded by anxiety or fear; we can learn to experience life as it is actually happening in the moment. We will discuss mindfulness later when I share about spirituality and connecting to your core beliefs.

The trauma of losing my husband shook my beliefs, and the growth that I experienced allowed me to begin developing new ways of thinking, and, in turn, to see new opportunities. But importantly, the opportunities did not just 'come'; I went to find them because, and by necessity, I expanded my thinking. I started thinking about what *is* possible. My goal was happiness, but I was terribly unhappy and scared. I decided to focus on what I could control. This is a very important concept. When we focus on the things we can control, we develop a sense of agency, which is connected to greater happiness and well-being and helps us to evaluate our choices and actions.

I became aware that I could have a say over *how* I framed what happened. I could not do anything about the fact that my husband was healthy one week and gone the next, but I could make meaning out of the experience. Heartbreak could not take that away from me. As Holocaust survivor and psychologist Viktor E. Frankl said, 'Everything can be taken from a man but one thing: the last of the human freedoms – to choose one's attitude in any given set of circumstances, to choose one's own way'. The bridge to happiness for me was finding my life purpose.

It was bad enough that my husband died; I decided that it would be terribly unfair and tragic for Ricardo to be wholly defined by his early death. So I chose to transform the pain into something hopeful, helpful and alive in WOHASU.

Four months after my husband passed, I showed up in Washington, not knowing anyone and unsure of what to expect. My family took turns accompanying me for the three weeks I had to spend in an intensive business-analytics course. The first day that I showed up to campus I was crying in the taxi because I realised that if I was there, it meant that my husband was not with us any more. I dried my tears and walked into the class and into the rest of my life. I felt like I was blindfolded, stepping into an open space and not knowing where my next step would fall.

I had a career in communications, but my husband was the primary financial provider. I now had to reinvent myself. Little did I know that I was reinventing myself from the inside. No one tells you that when you lose your spouse, you also lose your identity. I went from wife one minute to being single in another; I'd had a partner to raise our children, and suddenly I did not. I was like a newborn to a new and unwelcome reality, but I had very adult responsibilities.

Slowly, I was being transformed by learning new subjects like business analytics, where I had to study with intense focus because I didn't have a business or finance background. I became immersed in the subject, so much so that I tutored fellow students. This was my first experience in mindfulness; since it was so difficult for me, I had to be fully present to focus on learning the subject matter. Plus, I am dyslexic, and have to study even more to become proficient in something. But I wanted to do the programme, having decided that it was the crucial first step to my future and my goal of happiness – so I had to succeed. Being so engrossed in the subject allowed me time away from thinking about what had happened in the past and what dangers could be lurking in the future. I was fully present. I was in the moment, and it felt great. No fear. No anxiety.

With Ricardo's loss, my children no longer had a father, and my planned future, so carefully crafted in multiple conversations and concessions, was gone. We think that life owes us something, which will be delivered if we do this or pass on that. We bank on this, attaching dreams and stories that we rehearse in our minds. Often focusing on how it will be better in the future, not fully present in the moment, not savouring the now. But life doesn't really owe us anything. We are a collection of choices we make or fail to make. And yes, sometimes things do just happen, for no other reason than that they just happen.

The journey to the second part of my life had started and I had the goal that I set for myself: happiness.

Goal setting can be a very effective way to become motivated in the short term and hopeful about the future. According to researchers Edwin A. Locke and Gary P. Latham, the most effective goals should embody certain principles: clarity, challenge, commitment, feedback and complexity. Although this theory was originally applied to workplace performance, I applied it to my life. The researchers found that we are most successful when we pursue goals that have these characteristics. I certainly had a challenging and complex goal ahead of me, and I was 100 per cent committed because my children's future depended on my success. I listened to my body for feedback, to measure if I was going in the right direction. I gained clarity that learning something new like a business degree and meeting new people would not only expand but enrich my social network and thus increase my chances for happiness. Let's remember that the biggest influencer on our happiness is the state of our relationships.

We have 365 opportunities to start something new in a year (actually, more than that because we have the choice to start changing our mindsets and therefore our lives at any given moment). It is not easy, but it is possible. One of the most significant lessons that I learned is that life is not easy. Once I accepted that, life did, in fact, become much easier. Small steps towards change can look like waking up fifteen minutes earlier and prioritising your wellbeing by reading a few pages of an inspirational book, journalling about things that you are grateful for or that you are looking forward to doing, going for a walk or doing a short meditation. For example, a loving-kindness meditation can bring significant benefits to you and your relationships. According to Dr Emma Seppälä, Science Director of Stanford University's Center for Compassion and Altruism Research and Education, some of the benefits of this type of meditation can include feeling more positive emotions, fewer negative ones, less chronic pain and symptoms of post-traumatic stress disorder, increased social connection and it has even been shown to slow down ageing. These are all part of my morning routine. By taking these actions, I prime my brain towards the positive and start the day with a frame of mind that is receptive to noticing good things in my life and handling the challenges that any given day brings.

I didn't know it at the time, but I was developing a growth mindset which is necessary to see opportunities and new ways of being. According to Stanford professor

Carol Dweck: 'The growth mindset is based on the belief that your basic qualities are things you can cultivate through your efforts'. Conversely, a fixed mindset is one where you believe that the way you are born is set and cannot be changed – so you might think that you are a certain way because you were criticised as a child and therefore developed beliefs like 'I am opinionated and difficult'. Then you might act in ways that support these labels. A fixed mindset is limiting and allows very little room for new opportunities to blossom. But developing a new perspective through a growth mindset can be liberating because you are able to realise that labels are external – they're not your identity – and you can work on the skills that you do not yet have. In my case, I did not know how to be an entrepreneur. I knew very little about launching and running a business. But I knew I could learn how to do it. And that is what I did.

Humans are here to grow. We are continuously growing on a cellular level, nature is always growing, the seasons are changing . . . Life is an endless cycle of growth. It is natural that our minds can grow, too. And in fact, they do because of the neuroplasticity of the brain. The brain can change and adapt. Some of us may believe that the brain is fixed after childhood, but this is not the case. We can make new neural connections as reactions to experiences, but first, we need to become aware of this, understand how to go about it and then act in ways that reinforce the change we want. We can get better at doing things, we can develop new skills and we can become smarter. This is all part of the growth mindset, and it can happen because the brain is malleable. I experienced these mindset changes, and you can, too.

TIPS

1. Begin your day by thinking about your *to-be* list, not your *to-do* list. Reflect on how you want *to be* today.

2. Set goals that motivate you. Plan them out. Try to stick to the principles we discussed earlier in the chapter. Be specific. Instead of saying, 'I will start studying that topic', make a detailed plan: 'Tomorrow, at 7am, I will wake up and read for twenty minutes'. Try to stay emotionally committed to your goals.

3. Journal about your best future self. List three things that achieving your goal will allow you to do. Use your imagination; see yourself accomplishing your goals. Finally, to avoid losing motivation, track your progress. Small actions create big changes over time.

4. When faced with a challenge, explore what you can control in the situation. Ask yourself, 'What can I do about it? Can I take action? Am I reacting to an old frame or past experience, not what is really happening?'

PART 2

GREATER
PERSONAL
STRENGTH

4

JUST BREATHE – YOGA, STRESS AND STRENGTHS

'Breathe in deeply to bring your mind home to your body.'

Thich Nhat Hanh, Vietnamese monk and peace activist

The fastest reset that I have found to centre oneself is engaging in conscious breathing. Breathing is the only autonomic response that we can also purposely control. So many things happen right when you breathe correctly; and there are so many negative effects associated with breathing incorrectly.

I combine breathing exercises and meditation through practising yoga. This is another tool that has not only enhanced my life but has built my resilience in the face of adversity and gives me a boost when I want to feel more courageous. Thankfully, I had already been practising yoga for about fifteen years, when life happened. As I found myself in that cold ICU room, alarms beeping, human commotion all around me, losing my husband, I began to focus on my breath. His life was ending, and I survived that moment, literally one breath at a time. I kept repeating to myself: 'Just breathe'. Without this training, I would have probably collapsed.

Breathing brings you back to the now and grounds you on your feet. It's so disorienting to feel outside your body, and trauma can take you there. But taking a few deep breaths and listening to the sound of the air entering your nose and travelling through the back of your throat, feeling the expansion of your diaphragm and then back out again is so simple, yet so powerful. And it is available to all of us at any time. While short, shallow breathing can increase feelings of anxiety because it mimics the breathing we engage in when we are in fight-or-flight mode (see page 28), deep breathing sends signals to the brain that we are ok and safe because more oxygen is going to the thinking part of the brain. Some of the benefits of diaphragmatic breathing include lowering anxiety, blood pressure and heart rate, as well as improved decision making.

Yoga was important in finding my accidental happiness. I decided to try it after my mother repeatedly asked me to join her. I confess that I had preconceptions around it, and they were all negative. I only tried it so that my mom would stop telling me to. I'd practised sports all my life and I enjoy how exercise makes me feel, but I thought yoga would be too easy and a boring waste of time. The first time I tried it, I felt horrible. The instructor said that any beginners (which I was) should do the beginner options. Well, I was in great shape, so I thought, I'll show you who's a beginner! But it turned out I was embarrassed that I couldn't keep up, I wasn't very flexible and I learned that I didn't know how to breathe properly. I got a horrible headache; I absolutely hated it.

After my initial reaction, I decided I would try it three times, and then, if I still felt the same, I would never do it again. I was secretly hoping that I wouldn't enjoy it because liking it would prove my mom right. But I did it because I made the commitment to myself. I practised with humility as a beginner, developed proper breathing and fell in love with yoga. Thank you, Mom. Practising taught me balance – physical and emotional. Another tool in my toolbox to cultivate wellbeing.

According to the National Institutes of Health in the United States, yoga supports stress management, mental health, mindfulness, healthy eating, weight loss and quality sleep. Every morning, I practise at least one sun salutation and warrior series, so that I can reap the benefits of deep or diaphragmatic breathing, bringing my mind to the present moment, engaging my body in powerful poses and opening my heart to kindness. Before yoga, I did not know that I was breathing incorrectly. I was not aware of proper breathing: inhaling through the nose and bringing air all the way down towards the stomach, allowing the diagram to contract, belly to expand, filling the lungs with air. Now, I do breath exercises before any public speaking or when I am about to have a challenging conversation. It helps to calm my mind, so I can create more possibilities to be able to communicate my message and not get entangled in the emotions that I may be feeling in the moment or go into reaction mode if the other person responds in a way that is undesired.

When we face physical, mental or emotional challenges, our bodies activate our fight-or-flight stress response (see page 28). Everyone experiences stress; it is a stress response that gets us out of bed in the morning. But there are two main types of stress: eustress and distress. Eustress is the 'good' stress, as it is helpful for motivation, focus and energy; it is this type of stress that makes us pay special attention when driving at night on a low-lit road. It also serves us when we are facing certain challenges because it can compel us to act. But for stress to be beneficial it should also be manageable. Distress or 'bad' stress puts us in a place where we lack focus and motivation and it depletes our energy. It brings feelings of worry, doubt and anxiety; and when it is acute or chronic it can lead to illness, when we make poor lifestyle decisions like smoking and eating and drinking too much or not exercising enough.

Interestingly, many times it is how we think about stress that makes the difference in how we feel it, not the stress itself. This is another example of how we can control the way we experience life. When I feel stressed, I have decided to see it as a challenge. I ask myself: 'Is there something that I can learn from this experience or situation?' Perhaps it is as simple as understanding that the stressor in question is actually a motivator in disguise. What if what I thought was an obstacle was really a catalyst for change to help me accomplish my goals? When I started feeling anxious about what was necessary to successfully organise an international event with guests coming in from around the world, I learned that it served me to view each activity as taking me one step closer to delivering on my mission.

The ability to reframe how I view stress took me months to develop, but now, it is a helpful motivator. Viewing stress in this way, we learn that it signals what matters to us, is a tool for growth and sets our minds and bodies for important tasks.

It is very important to understand that sometimes it is not stress that is damaging, but the absence of recovery time. Think of all the times you've made great excuses for skipping a meal or exercise because you didn't have enough time, or when you've cut down on sleep to meet a deadline, making you sleep-deprived. In the long run, these 'shortcuts' backfire on our health and wellbeing. Needless to say, we are not happy campers.

Difficult moments can be overwhelming, and the intensity of emotions comes in waves, which is why rest and recovery are particularly important during these times. We can therefore decide to implement periods for recovery throughout our days, weeks and years. These can become interwoven into the fabric of our lives to prevent chronic stress. There are 'micro-', 'mid-' and 'macro-' recovery levels, all of which can help us to feel replenished and reduce the chances of burnout. Deep-belly breathing, movement and body awareness are examples of a micro-level relaxation response that can counter distress. Mid-level recovery examples are healthy eating, exercise and sleep. Vacations are macro-level recovery and can promote health and success.

Managing stress and taking care of our health are significant steps towards becoming happier. But there is another practice that research has shown to increase happiness, motivation and meaning, and that is identifying and using your character strengths. Research has found that tackling our weaknesses through a strengths-based approach can be helpful. Strengths are our innate capacities for particular ways of thinking, feeling and behaving. They are a combination of what we are naturally good at and what we have learned during our lives.

Strengths spotting can enhance personal and professional success. I learned to take a strengths-based approach to my life, which has been useful in building up my self-esteem. We all have strengths and the mix of these is part of what makes each of us wonderfully unique. By being more connected with ourselves and choosing elements that embody the best of us, we can feel more empowered and gain a greater sense of agency, thus increasing goal-setting behaviour. Life then doesn't have to happen accidentally. Using a strengths perspective, we can begin to plan our lives, and gain motivation to accomplish our goals.

There are several ways that you can identify your strengths. You might want to take a survey like the ones listed at the end of this chapter (see page 55); or you can explore times when you felt that you were in flow and notice which parts of you were shining in those moments. During a state of flow, you lose all concept of time, the activity difficulty matches the level of your ability and you find enjoyment for its own sake. In other words, you are fully engaged in and motivated by what you are doing. Another way to start recognising your strengths is by asking people you trust. What do *they* think you are very good at? Their comments might provide insights you were previously unaware of.

Another way to cultivate happiness is to choose a profession that works to your strengths. I could have decided to work in finance or technology, but I am not particularly good at either. Instead, through entrepreneurship, I created a business where I can play to my strengths: courage, curiosity, creativity and love. This way, I can fulfil my purpose and experience flow at work, which increases my productivity, sense of engagement and creative energy. In exposing and using our strengths, not only can we experience more moments of flow, but we can also become the best versions of ourselves.

TIPS

1. Identify and name your stress; do not suppress it. What are your feelings telling you? Own your stress, as it signals something that is important in your life. Evaluate if you can identify your stress response as helpful for performance – it can be redefined as an 'alarm' or motivator for accomplishing something towards your goal. If, for example, you are stressed about an upcoming exam you haven't prepared for, listen to that 'alarm', and react constructively by getting down to some studying.

2. Think of how you would like your life to be. Come up with a plan to help you get there. Which areas of wellbeing do you need to work on? What skills do you need to learn? Which strengths do you want to develop? You might want to take a strengths survey like: Via Character Strengths Survey https://www.viacharacter.org/ or Strength Profile: https://www.strengthsprofile.com/

3. Identify times when you are in a state of flow. What were you doing? Were you alone or in a group? What conditions placed you in flow? Using this information, make a plan to create more opportunities to experience flow.

5

KEEP MOVING

'Each individual will approach the path to
wellness a bit differently, but it starts with getting
in touch with your own mind and body in a kind
and meaningful way.'

Dr Lakshmi Menezes, MD, internal medicine physician

Walking with grief is difficult. Sitting with loss is worse.
But how do you process the fact that your husband – a
dynamic, big, strong guy – got sick and died of the flu
within a period of ten days? You don't move on easily
from losing the love of your life. You learn to live with
the loss because it is too painful to stay stuck. I prefer
action.

We have all experienced challenges in our lives, and
it takes courage to let go. It's the hero who chooses life,
but that only comes after we accept that no matter how
many tears we shed, the past will not change.

Growth requires movement, which can be physical or mental. We need both, and they are linked through the mind–body connection. The mind interacts with the body and the body interacts with the mind, providing constant feedback which can generate a positive or negative impact.

One of the pillars of happiness is physical wellbeing. I always try to keep that in mind, especially when I am very busy and don't have much discretionary time. But much of my work involves meetings, travel and writing, sometimes leaving little room for exercise and to connect with the messages that my body is giving me.

To pre-empt a possible lack of movement during my day, I do a ten-minute yoga routine in the morning before starting my work day. The way you move (say, with different poses) can affect the way you feel. When I skip exercise or sit for too long, my mood and energy suffer. Sometimes, you can change your mental state just by changing your posture. Yoga is a great way to move your body through powerful poses and engaging in deep breathing.

It's interesting that when I have a lot going on is when I need exercise the most, but it's also when I am at the greatest risk of not doing it. This is one of the tendencies that I am trying to work on. If I'm writing for long periods of time, I make an effort to get up from my desk every two hours and go for a walk. Even a short one, just around the block, is enough to help me feel more energised and focused. Exercising outdoors packs a double benefit because being in nature increases positive emotions, as does physical activity.

Some people turn up the music and dance a little. Others go for a run or jog. Everything works – no matter what you do, there are certain biological changes that happen when you move. Exercise bumps up the production of your brain's feel-good hormones (endorphins), lowers cortisol levels, improves brain health, helps manage weight, reduces the risk of disease and strengthens bones and muscles. Here we are letting biology do the 'heavy lifting' by naturally helping us to feel better. Exercise is a definite *go to* if you want to feel happier.

Mental 'movement' is also extremely important to cultivating happiness. Here, I am referring to engaging in flexible thinking and fostering a growth mindset. I realised the power of movement when I started traveling back and forth between Miami and Washington. I was changing physical locations every other week. I was in motion, jumping on a plane, experiencing a new city and meeting new people – but I was also shifting my mindset away from what I lost to what I could gain. Everything was new. How could I protect my children from the impact of 'the situation'? How could I provide the best life possible for us three? What was the 'best' life, anyway? I had to learn all kinds of new things because the life I knew had ended. Countless times I thought, What the heck am I doing and where am I going? Answer: I don't know, but I am going to figure it out. And where exactly am I going? *I am going to happiness.*

It is important not to get stuck in our thoughts, especially when they are negative, useless or, even worse, toxic. We all have thoughts that we cannot control. And when we experience any kind of loss – whether a person, a job, an opportunity, a house – it is easy to get stuck in grief, longing, remorse, regret or, especially, the most common of them all: the atrocious 'What if . . . ?' The 'What if . . . ?' is a game that plays out in our brains – a bit like the sirens' song that tries to lure us. It is a temptation focused on a false sense of control, as if we could go back and change the past.

I danced with the 'What if . . . ?' for a while. For two years, in fact, on and off. My useless thought was: *what if* I had taken Ricardo to a different hospital? But nothing good can come from dwelling on that thought. First, I can't take him to a different hospital now – that, obviously, can never happen – so what is the point of dwelling on it? Second, that thought added to the injury I already felt. It was not helpful and there was nothing I could do about it.

Sometimes we can do something to change the things we feel bad about, and here, our mental struggles might even be helpful. The right dose of anxiety, for instance, can be extremely helpful when you have a deadline: yes, you feel uneasy, nervous, maybe you can't sleep well, but you also feel the urgency to act and, by doing so, you meet that deadline or catch that flight. In my case, however, the hospital thought would never bring change, only regret. I decided to move away from it and then, whenever it came back into my mind, I moved again and again, until now I don't think about that any more.

It is the nature of the mind to wander, so thoughts will come in and out of our brains, like waves crashing against the shore, and there's nothing we can do to stop them. In fact, it is healthy not to block them, but at the same time not to be swept away by them. Instead, we can view them as data points giving us information. The hospital thought for me was a reminder that I cannot control the past, and trying to do so is counterproduct- ive to my wellbeing in the present.

When we get stuck in negative-thinking cycles, it is like a tidal pond on the beach: with no new water coming in, it stagnates; but when the ocean replenishes it with fresh water, it revives and brings new life. Similarly, by practising fluid thinking, transitioning from one thought to another, we can make space for fresh, new ones. We are mentally 'moving', like we do physically. I am not saying this is easy. In fact, it can be quite difficult because fear, anxiety and loneliness can paralyse our physical and mental movement. Sometimes we sit with our feelings and that's ok, but we also need to know when to get up. Keep in mind that when we are sad, the last thing we want to do is go outside, dance, exercise or be grateful and positive. I have been there. But I learned not to wait until I wanted to do these things, choosing instead to do them anyway, like a discipline. We don't think about the benefits of brushing our teeth and we don't ask ourselves if we want to do it. We simply do so out of habit and because we want healthy teeth and gums and fresh breath.

Another example of thought movement is when I got home from the hospital the day that Ricardo passed away. The second thing I did, after hugging my son, was to throw away my husband's toothbrush and shaving cream. I had to move my thinking from 'he is alive' to 'he is not coming back'. This might seem like an extreme reaction on my side because it was so soon, but I was very attached to being his wife, and I knew intuitively that I had to start understanding that he was gone in order to figure out how to start a new reality.

I imagine that many people have felt something similar when a relationship has ended and one person has left the other, or when they have experienced any other form of grief. The identify shift that grief brings can be very challenging and impactful. No two people grieve the same way and I found that there are no neat stages to follow. There are many difficult emotions, thoughts and decisions that only get easier with time. The timing of when we do certain things, however, is subjective. The important thing to hold on to is that we can focus on what went right in the past, on what we have power to change in the now and what we plan for in the future. My husband, who was a doctor, used to say, 'Healing sometimes takes a tincture of time'.

If you look at the research on memory, you will find that we remember the peak of experiences that we go through. For example, if we go on a two-week holiday, most of us will not remember every moment. The brain cannot store all the experiences we've had, so we remember the peaks, whether good or bad, and the ending. Of course, losing my husband was a peak experience for me – not in a good way, but for sure one that stuck out. The silver lining of this mechanism is that post-traumatic growth is a resetting experience. In the past, I would ask myself things like, 'Did I wear the right thing?' 'Did I say the right thing?' 'Was my presentation ok?' I cared a lot about things like this, and from time to time, I still have these thoughts, like anybody else. But I don't give them so much attention or importance any more. To me, they are trivial things that don't deserve much of my energy.

In other words, I have become more resilient. Like

everyone, I experience moments of regret, but I have developed what I call 'mind movement'. It is easier for me to transition from thought to thought and not to get stuck because I am aware of how depleting thinking traps can be, taking away happiness and creating clouds of darkness. When these unwelcome thoughts pop up, I tell myself, 'Ok, you can let them go now or you can indulge them' – but I know they can act like sugar for my brain, providing little nourishment, just empty calories. So to avoid getting stuck, I impose a time limit: I give myself five minutes to ruminate or complain, then I move. I don't shut off how I feel; I just choose where to focus my energy, actions and thoughts. I've learned to slow down my thinking so that I become aware of the choices at my disposal: what can I do? What do I control? This way, I can make decisions that are more helpful to me and get me closer to my goals and how I want to feel.

Keep in mind that the journey is not linear. It has bumps and dips and valleys along the way, and that is ok. The important thing to remember is that we are trending upwards along the 'happiness' ladder and working towards our life goals while investing in social relationships and finding fulfilment along the way. There will be setbacks – some that we bring about ourselves and others that are outside our control and come from life events that just happen. I dared to love again and got my heart broken as an example. But if you stay in the moment and use the tools that you have identified as helpful to you, you will realise that you are essentially ok and can find a way to feel well and become happier.

I am still *becoming*. But I found where happiness is. It is inside me. Happiness begins inside and moves out, rippling to others.

TIPS

1. Try to maintain a healthy relationship with your problems and put them in perspective. Remember to also look out for the good that happens every day. Talk and journal about it; this way, you expand on the things that go right in your life.

2. Put your favourite music on and dance. If you work from home, go out for a five-minute walk every few hours – you can set a timer to help with this. Remember, going outdoors and being in nature has great benefits.

3. Notice what triggers you to get stuck in negative thinking patterns. Can you see them coming? List two things that you can do to counter this.

6

LETTING GO OF PAIN TO MAKE SPACE FOR GROWTH

'When you numb your pain you also numb your joy.'

Brené Brown, American professor

Happiness needs space to grow.

Many of us experience moments when we feel it is time for something new or we sense a calling to evolve into someone new. For that to happen, we must let go of the old.

For me, this started one year after Ricardo passed away. I was with a group of friends at Georgetown when I heard a joke. It was a really funny one. Nevertheless, I didn't laugh. I felt a sense of distance and judgment. I found myself analysing and asking myself whether a widow 'should' laugh. And at that moment, I had a revelation: I was going to embrace life and I would give myself permission to laugh again.

When we go through a difficult time, it's important not to minimise things. That's true. But at the same time, we should feel what we are feeling, especially if it is a positive emotion. Challenging life events leave scars in our lives, but we should remember that they are *not* our lives. They are things that *happened in* our lives. We must make space in our minds, and in our hearts, for happiness – not forced, but natural happiness. That does not mean we should dismiss challenging feelings. Rather, that we accept the full gamut of human emotions, including laughter for a widow. We should not be afraid to be happy and, if possible, not be afraid to feel sadness either. Life has room for both, and there is much we can do to increase our happiness and the happiness of others. It starts by making space for it.

After my loss, I found that some people, even friends, assumed that I should behave in certain ways. Interestingly, these opinions came from people who had not gone through a similar experience but had formed expectations based on their own limiting beliefs. If we are struggling, there's a chance that people we know may treat us differently. Chances are that they don't mean to hurt us; they are just treating us according to their pre-set frames of reference, or they might be afraid of the emotions that can arise as a result of our challenge. Often, they are well-meaning people, who react through their own lenses. In other words, they want us to be 'predictable' in our behaviour, which means fitting the paradigm that makes them feel a little more comfortable. That does not mean we must conform. When we are going through difficult times, we are aware that something feels 'off' in our lives, that we are 'outside the pack'. To heal, we need to go in the opposite direction, by being with people who help to increase our sense of belonging and who accept us unconditionally. We need to be seen for who we are, not what happened to us. When something traumatic happens, we crave normalcy, so non-judgment, including no self-judgment, is especially important. We need to give ourselves time to process our situations and accept the changes we might be going through internally.

We do not have to act in a way that has been prescribed by others to fit a mould. In the same way that we should not suppress sadness, we should not suppress happiness. If we smile, wear a red dress or go out for dinner with friends, it does not mean we no longer feel the impact of the challenge. We are going to feel it as long as we feel it. In some cases, a lifetime. But we can learn to live with it in ways that don't impede our well-being and can even provide opportunities for growth.

One of the most important things to do to become

happier is to feel *all* emotions, including the 'negative' ones, like emotional pain, disappointment, anger and loss. In the right context, they can even be helpful. According to Dr Barbara Fredrickson's Broaden-and-Build model, negative emotions can be very useful by allowing us to narrow our focus and take specific actions – like leaving a relationship (romantic or professional) that is toxic, for example. We might be struggling with which decisions to take, but feeling our challenging feelings can help us to focus on how/when to leave and take the necessary action for our health and wellbeing. When we block our feelings, they grow. So if we resist emotional pain, well, then, that grows, too. Think of it this way: if I ask you not to think of a pink elephant, what happens? The image of a pink elephant pops into your brain. It is the same concept with negative emotions. The key is not to dwell.

It is also important to understand that we don't have to act on all our emotions. Feelings are feelings – they are not *right* or *wrong*. Action is what creates the consequences which can be beneficial or not, to us and others. We can feel our feelings and let them go; we do not have to act. We can choose to entertain those that are either helpful by providing important data or those that generate a sense of wellbeing, harmony, contentment, meaning, gratitude or joy. Creating an environment where happiness can flourish in our lives requires learning to let go of thoughts, beliefs or emotions that don't serve us. It is important to feel all our emotions and then, equally important to let some go.

There are many things that I had to learn to let go. The first step was deciding that *I wanted* to let go. But in order to do so, I had to identify what I wanted to release.

Deciding to move on from the life that I had known for over two decades to creating a new self took more courage than I knew I had. I was very vulnerable, but I had an open mind. At first, it was only slightly open, but as I acted, I became more open-minded. In doing I was becoming. By focusing on selecting thoughts that were aligned with my values and purpose, I began to envision a way out. And I was doing this on my own. Would I have got another master's degree, started a business and built a movement in the past? I don't think so. And looking back, it feels risky to have completely changed my life, career, home and identity. Yet I was not scared at the time because I knew I had to move on.

Letting go of the pain and other emotions can be hard because, at times, they are like a worn blanket that gives us comfort because we are so habituated to its presence. But there is a price to be paid here – because holding on can rob us of our energy, leaving us depleted, with little room for happiness to take root. For me, the pain had become a reminder of Ricardo, and I had to let that go. I feared that through this process, I would remember him less. And sometimes we do that: we keep rehashing painful memories so that we can remain 'close' to a person. But in letting Ricardo go, he became part of my life in a new way. I do things that I know he would like, and I get satisfaction from doing them because it gives me an opportunity to remember him, and smile. For example, I used to leave dirty dishes on the sink soaking overnight which would bother him (even though he never told me; he just did them himself, which bothered me because I felt guilty!). I don't leave the dishes out any more, and I think of him as I am doing them. I also used to place the toilet paper one way, and he another. Now, I choose to do it the way he did it and I smile. Small things, yet they create opportunities for intimate remembrance in my daily life; and that makes me happy.

Practising emotional agility is another way to create space between the thinker and the thoughts. Harvard psychologist Susan David's groundbreaking research on emotional agility shows that the way we think about our thoughts and emotions influences our happiness, well-being, relationships and success. Emotions come and go like waves in the ocean. It is helpful to see them as information – not as *good* or *bad*, but rather as guideposts to actions or reminders of something that we need to do or accept and move on. This is why it is so important not to say, 'I am angry', 'I am disappointed' or 'I am sad', but rather, 'I feel angry', 'I feel disappointed' or 'I feel sad'. I learned that by using labelling, we learn to see our thoughts and feelings as fleeting – as sources of data that are sometimes helpful and sometimes not. *We* are not anger, disappointment or sadness. These are feelings, not identities. Without this awareness, we might find ourselves in a tsunami of thoughts and emotions, which can create havoc in our personal and professional lives, leaving unintended consequences around our actions. But with this simple reframe and labelling exercise, we are able to create space and distance between our identities and our feelings, so that we can go beyond action and reaction. We become aware that we are what we habitually identify with, good or bad, helpful or harmful.

When we let go of disappointment, we make room for good things to happen in our lives. By creating distance between our emotions, thoughts and reactions we gain a new viewpoint from which to better evaluate our opportunities. It is in this 'space' that we can see we have a choice over our perceptions and resulting actions. This is where happiness can happen. The ability to see my opportunities allowed me to feel a greater sense of personal strength, one that has evolved into courage which I use to accomplish my job and show love to my family, friends and even strangers. Today, I travel around the world engaging in public speaking, something I used to be nervous about doing and therefore avoided. I am able to share my personal story, talk about the global happiness movement and discuss the science of happiness because I let go of the pain. These experiences have empowered me and allowed me to feel more courageous as I am doing them.

In later chapters, we will see ways in which we can create space for happiness by being kind, forgiving, loving and grateful. These ways of being can be learned and cultivated and, when practised, can increase positive emotions as a powerful by-product. According to Fredrickson's theory: 'Cultivated positive emotions not only counteract negative emotions, but also broaden individuals' habitual modes of thinking and build their personal resources for coping'. Opening up to positive emotions allowed me a broader view of the choices available to me. For example, I could invest my money in creating a happiness company, I could grow a movement, I could travel with my friends, I could go on a date, I could cry and then smile. I could grow from trauma.

Conversely, thinking hooks and emotional rigidity can do the opposite. When we get stuck in negative thinking patterns our choices and happiness diminish. The first step is to become aware of these hooks. One way to identify that we are stuck is when we think the same thing over and over again. It's like jumping on a hamster wheel to nowhere. I know that's where I am when I have repetitive thoughts that cause me to feel anxious or fearful. One of my recurring thoughts was, How am I going to take care of my kids by myself? I became aware that I had to get out of that thinking pattern because it was depleting my much-needed energy, interfering with my problem-solving skills and impacting my sleep, as well as limiting my choices because I was in a cycle of anxiety.

A great way to test whether you are hooked in a negative thought pattern is to evaluate your sleep. Are you able to fall asleep, stay asleep overnight and do you feel rested when you wake? I had many sleepless nights, until I was able to get off that hamster wheel of negative thought patterns and switch to the more positive thinking that allowed me to make the decision to attend Georgetown.

Finally, Carol Dweck's work on growth mindsets really helped me to understand that looking at life through a lens of growth and learning takes away bitterness, unforgiveness and blame. What I have learned is that growth is always there for us, especially after failure. Life provides us with so many opportunities, big and small, to evolve and transform. Growth can be uncomfortable, and we might not be very happy while it's happening – but that is ok. It is scary to let go of old identities but becoming can be a period of discovery and opportunity to live life more fully. It's a bit like when the earthbound, lowly caterpillar evolves into the beautiful butterfly that takes flight. When I let go of the pain, I gained the ability to see my choices. I chose happiness.

TIPS

1. Watch Susan David's TED Talk on Emotional Agility.

2. Exercise: recognise your thought patterns – where are you stuck? Label your thoughts and emotions ('I am feeling . . .', 'I am thinking . . .') Accept all your emotions/thoughts, recognise that they are transient and take action that aligns with your values.

3. Try to surround yourself with people who are optimistic and positive. Happiness is contagious. You can recognise them by how you feel when you are with them. Do you feel energy rich or poor after spending time together?

4. Identify areas in your life where you would like to let go of a fixed mindset and move towards a growth mindset. What is one thing that you can let go of? What small step can you take now? Write a sticky note and post it on your bathroom mirror to remind you of the reframe. For example, if you feel inadequate managing your money, you might take an online course on money management. Understand the myth around your belief and then work on letting it go. Accept that doing something new might be uncomfortable at first. That is natural; try it anyway.

PART 3

NEW
APPRECIATION
OF LIFE

7

SAVOURING AND STUFF THAT MAKES ME HAPPY, JUST BECAUSE . . .

'There is a great beauty in little things.'
Mehmet Murat ildan, Turkish playwright

I really love to talk about things that make me happy – things I don't have to think about, but just feel. You might believe that savouring the moments that make your life special is trivial, but these are the experiences that create a strong foundation for the resilience we need to foster in our ever-changing physical and emotional environments. And savouring or paying attention to the glimmers (moments that spark joy or awe – the opposite of triggers) in our lives also cultivates our happiness.

These moments can be extra special when we share them with others, which is important because strong relationships are significant drivers of wellbeing.

I have a very deep and long-lasting relationship that has given me great comfort during painful and lonely times. We have long conversations, and even though I am the only one speaking, I know he listens. I have enjoyed immensely the presence, loyalty and companionship that my almost-twenty-year-old Shih Tzu, Junior Guggenheim, has brought to my life. He has made me laugh, elevating my serotonin levels and endearing him forever to my heart and soul. I savour the memories of our interactions and enjoy the play in the now.

The benefits of pet ownership are enjoyed by millions of people around the world. Actually, pets, especially dogs, provided many people companionship during the COVID-19 pandemic. In fact, according to science, pets help to relieve loneliness, stress and anxiety (all of which I have experienced in varying degrees since 'the event'), and they also make us more social by expanding our connections to others and helping us make more friends. As a matter of fact, our dog is a conversation starter wherever we take him. Very few dogs are twenty years old. Plus, he is super cute.

Junior is especially significant to my family because we have many stories featuring him and Ricardo. Sadly, the dog has been with my children longer than their father was; happily, he has lived well beyond his life expectancy and his presence helped to soothe us in our grief. Both are true; I choose to focus on the latter. We have a collection of sweet and loving moments that contribute to family stories and collective memories of life with Ricardo. In a way, when Junior passes those stories will surely evolve into more memories for our bittersweet library of gems that make life worth living. Still, even though I know better, I try to avoid the feelings that will come from the loss of our beloved dog. Then, I become aware and focus on how wonderful it is to have him and how he has enriched our lives and impacted our happiness. Just thinking about him brings a smile to my face.

We know from the Happiness Research Institute in Denmark that people are happier if they hold a positive, nostalgic view of the past. I know that I will remember playful moments with Junior with nostalgia, and I certainly will savour memories of this special dog, which is great, because according to happiness researcher Meik Wiking, good memories strengthen our identity, improve our sense of purpose and fortify our relationships. Memories are reminders of who we are.

I choose to think about the joy of having Junior now and will deal with what comes when it comes. We cannot outrun life, and trying to do so can only bring problems. Frequently, we bypass feeling good in the moment because we know that it will end. Well, everything ends. That is the nature of life. There are seasons for everything. If we neglect noticing the good in the present, we risk perceiving only one side of reality, which can leave us missing significant moments. Many cultures even believe that saying you are having a great day or that you are very happy can bring bad luck!

If, instead, we can be courageous to also experience happiness and joy – and to express them when they are happening, we will gain a balanced outlook on life. For most of us, life could be better or worse, but in the now, we are ok; we are mostly well at this moment. In Chapter 5, we talked about focusing on what went right in the past, but something we can all do as well is to look at what is going right in our lives now, in the present. We can do this on purpose, and many times we need to do it with much effort because we have developed ineffective thinking patterns that have become second nature to us. As mentioned earlier, remember what the happiness experts say: when we appreciate the good, the good appreciates. Whatever we pay attention to grows. So if you notice the good happening right before your eyes, it grows because you are more aware of these positive moments. By scanning for good things, activities and relationships that bring a sense of satisfaction, harmony and peace, we feel better. We see, for example, that nature is one of the most powerful tools we have at our disposal. Research has confirmed that being out-doors can help us feel greater cohesiveness with people around us, inspire better communication, increase cre-ativity and – maybe most importantly – nature can help us to develop our characters and confidence. Taking advantage of this precious tool is easy and costs noth-ing. Look for beauty and try to experience a sense of awe when you are in nature. Try to be in nature for around 120 minutes a week to reap the maximum bene-fits to wellbeing. This can include taking a walk in the woods, going to a park or even viewing something out-side your own front door. It doesn't matter how you make up your 120 minutes; it is the accumulated time that matters.

It's funny – I was living in an apartment where I could see the most amazing sunsets, but I only noticed this when the pandemic stopped my travels. I thought to myself, Who put that sunset there? Of course, it was there all along, but I had never paid attention to it. It's so true that all too often we just don't notice the aston-ishing things or people right in front of our eyes. Slowing down gave me the opportunity to pan out my focus and see beauty around me.

Happiness is expansive. Since it takes more effort to remember positive events, invest in being fully present for the good things that happen. When we fail to notice, it is like the event didn't happen because we construct our lives through perception. But the wonderful thing is that when we change our outlook, we change our lives.

Music provides another opportunity for savouring. Listening to music can invite a cascade of emotions and memories, creating a mindset shift almost as soon as we listen to the first lyrics or notes. Music activates most regions in the brain, beginning with the auditory cortex; it activates and synchronises the areas related to emotion and memory and it engages the motor system, even before there is physical movement – all of which makes it a great pairing with exercise. Music provides a full brain workout. Savouring music became an important part of my daily routine after Ricardo died. Music brings me a diversity of memories that generate pleasure, nostalgia, sweet melancholy and sometimes mischief. I like to listen to traditional rock and roll from the past when I'm in search of deep thinking. I listen to 80s music when I'm in a funk. I can't listen to one of my husband's favourites, Seal. *Yet.* And Pearl Jam and Bob Marley saved my life the first year after he passed: every morning when I showered and prepared for my day (each of which felt insurmountable, like it would last a year), I played their songs. I didn't know it at the time, but I was using something that research shows helps to elevate our happiness. I did it daily and made it a habit, adding another tool to my happiness practice. Slowly making progress towards happiness, inching my way there. The adage that small actions over time create big change is true. I still listen to music when I am getting ready for the day. It has become automatic; I do not wait to *want* to do it. I do it as a health habit because I know that it elevates my mood. I just do it, like the Nike slogan.

It's important to choose the music that puts you in a better mood. We are all different and react to different music in different ways. What is lovely to one person may be annoying to another. We are our own experts about what makes us happy. But listening to music can provide many benefits and all we have to do is listen; biology does the rest! Some other great reasons for adding more music to our lives are that it has been found to reduce anxiety, blood pressure and pain, while also improving sleep quality, mood, mental alertness and memory. This is low-hanging fruit for feeling better with minimal effort.

Connecting with what makes us happy is a great guide to creating a life plan. In developing awareness of actions that improve our wellbeing, we are creating a more conducive environment for our happiness to grow. We plan most things in our lives, but we do not plan for our wellbeing because society largely prioritises productivity. We measure the success of countries, organisations and people by how productive they are. As a social entrepreneur, who is totally committed to WOHASU's mission, even I sometimes work seven days a week; I am getting better about this, but it is an area that still needs improvement. So I am investing in having more of a personal life as part of my life plan. I am also deciding which city to live in which has the best life/work integration for me.

It feels strange now to reflect on how I used to expect to be happy without any direction or participation from me. I wanted a 'great' life. But guess what? I *had* a great life. I know that now, but back then I was focused on all the things I didn't have. I felt disappointment and sometimes boredom as I waited for something external to happen so that I could feel happier. These events came but they were sporadic, and I didn't know how to be sustainably happy. I had a specific mindset of what happiness was *supposed* to look like and little understanding of how much satisfaction and happiness could come from living a purpose-driven life.

I don't know why we leave the most important aspect of our lives – how we feel in and with them – to chance. We behave as if the biggest source of our happiness is external. We wait and wait and wait. But happiness flows from the inside out, so we don't have to wait any more. Searching for happiness outside ourselves leaves us feeling empty because we never quite get there; we will always be pursuing.

We might think that things like taking the time to listen to music, walk in nature, laugh with friends, hug our families, pet our dogs or eat away from our desks are not productive, but we now have enough evidence to show they improve our wellbeing, which also makes us more productive in the long term. Happiness leads to success in all areas of life – from work to relationships and health – not the other way around.

In reframing challenges as exploration and learning and noticing the wonderful moments that bring meaning to our lives, we are able to become happier. We can also celebrate 'average' experiences by elevating the meaning that we attach to them. For example, that beautiful sunset I mentioned earlier: obviously, sunsets happen daily – nothing could be more average or normal than that. But by taking the time to actually *see* the sun setting, and perhaps sharing the moment with a friend or loved one, we expand the moment and make it special. It has the potential to become a peak experience of our day. We can create extraordinary moments out of the ordinary, and when we experience awe, our wellbeing improves.

As a by-product of living with me, my sons have

learned my happiness strategies, too. Sometimes I am *very* annoying. I wake up in the morning, and – especially on days when I feel down – I sing and dance in front of them. I am a very bad singer, but I sing to them, 'I love you, I love you, I love you'. They ask, 'What's wrong with you?' But, by then, I feel so much better. I am laughing at myself and laughing with them.

Humour is a wonderful remedy for a bad mood. It reduces stress, helps us connect with each other and releases endorphins (those feel-good hormones). It's important to note that we can experience different emotions almost simultaneously in response to one event – pain and laughter can coexist. For example, my friend has a very cynical sense of humour, which helped her to process her father's death. There is also research showing that laughter can lessen physical pain and even improve the immune system. Humour is another skill that we can develop. For me, it is very helpful to use it when I am anxious or feeling a bit overwhelmed. I find that it releases the intensity of the feeling by changing my perspective when I feel that I am getting stuck in a negative thinking pattern. And laughter is contagious, which is wonderful. My husband was very funny, and I think that is one of the things that really connected us. Today, I use humour during work meetings; it often contributes to finding increased common ground for collaboration and it helps to take the stress out of a difficult conversation. It's also a great tool to use with our children, bringing more joy into the relationship.

All that said, it is also important to note that humour should never belittle, offend or come at someone else's expense.

Even a simple smile can make a positive impact. The physical act of smiling can have great benefits due to the release of neurotransmitters serotonin and dopamine which can improve mood. It is a good way to 'hack' our systems when we are in a funk. And it's good for the receiver, too. Being aware of this, I make it a habit now to smile at strangers or when meeting someone new. It's amazing how positively people react, becoming kinder and more helpful. I also remind myself to smile when I am giving a presentation. Sometimes, when I get very involved in the subject, I become intense. But when I smile, I relax, improving my delivery. Plus, it signals the audience to join me on the journey as I share my message.

Play is a great way to welcome laughter into our lives. We do not play enough as adults. And sadly, children are engaging in less 'unstructured play' every year. But we can do something about it. Instead of using social media or television as a distraction in the evenings, we can play. Research shows that play can help to regulate emotions and enhance problem solving by activating the prefrontal cortex in the brain. Clearly, including play as part of our plan has significant positive biological effects.

Play time for adults also helps us to stay young. When we play, we are exercising our brains by giving them opportunities to be more creative and learn something new. Play can also strengthen our relationships by increasing feelings of connection with friends or colleagues. And it can even help to heal emotional wounds. I think that is why I am so playful when I am feeling overwhelmed.

Another opportunity to improve our physical and mental health and one that involves savouring is eating. We taste our food, but we can savour the textures and richness of what we are consuming and, importantly, we can also savour the conversations and interactions with the people at our tables. Since we are what we eat, we should pay close attention to what we consume. Recent findings show that our mental states can be impacted by our gut health, and that there is a bidirectional link between the brain, gut and microbiome called the gut–brain axis. It seems that people suffering with anxiety and depression might benefit from adding probiotics to their diets, as well as eating nutrient-dense foods, also making mindful eating a wise choice. Breaking bread with others around the table makes us feel happier and more satisfied with life, and increases social bonding by generating greater trust in others and more engagement with our communities. It can also be a lot of fun and bring much laughter, thus strengthening our social connections.

Little things that at first seem ordinary and trivial have the power of adding significance and meaning to our lives, making us happier. So we can see that how we spend our time matters to our wellbeing. Or perhaps, how we *think* about how we spend our time is what matters. According to time and happiness researcher Dr Cassie Holmes, the way we think about how much time we have is what creates the difference between feeling time rich versus time poor. Her research found that we need between two and five hours of discretionary time every day for optimal wellbeing. These are the times when we are most likely to savour life. Below two hours' discretionary time is not enough to do the things we enjoy, while, interestingly, more than five decreases our happiness because we feel a diminished sense of purpose.

Time is our most valuable resource, yet we don't know how much we have, so we need to plan how we use it, otherwise we can feel like we have wasted it. And research shows that people feel worse about losing time than losing money. (We can always make more money; we cannot make more time.)

So now that we understand more about savouring, we can begin to develop a life plan that includes moments for creating daily encounters that count. This way, we can elevate our moods by raising our awareness of the special things resulting from 'ordinary' interactions and activities, as well as the natural setting outside our doors. Many times, just noticing the ordinary makes it extraordinary. Life provides us with ample opportunities. Be curious, find them and share them.

TIPS

1. Make it a point not to eat at your desk or in front of the television. Create a special dining environment at least once a week. Remember that you get to define what 'special' is to you. Create something meaningful, and savour it with others.

2. Pay attention to how your body feels with different music or songs. Make a playlist of the songs that make you feel good. Play it daily for a week. Evaluate how that feels.

3. If you are feeling time poor, track how you are spending your time. Cassie Holmes has a great time-tracking exercise along with time sheets on her website: www.cassiemholmes.com/timecrafting

PART 4

RELATIONSHIPS

8

LOVE, CONNECTION AND RELATIONSHIPS

'To practice the art of loving we have first to choose love – admit to ourselves that we want to know love and be loving.'

bell hooks, American author

Why is it that scientists have done so little research on love, while volumes have been written about war? Maybe because it's difficult to measure the impact of love as opposed to war, or because pop culture has reduced love to an idyllic romantic notion, where only one person can fill the *love space* in our lives. Yet few emotions are more important than love to our individual and collective wellbeing. When understood correctly, we see that, in fact, as American psychiatry professor and author Daniel J. Siegel puts it, 'the health of our lives depends on the love in our relationships'.

Love saved my life.

My love for others, especially for my sons, and their love for me changed the trajectory of my life from grief to happiness. After they lost their father, I realised that to help my sons, I had to become whole again, but I didn't know how to do that. Because of my love for them, I chose something radical. I chose happiness. I desperately wanted to make a situation that could never be ok, better.

One of the most difficult aspects of what happened is that through a mother's love, I had always wanted to protect my children from the harsh realities of life. I was like a lioness protecting her cubs. But then came the reality that in this case I could not fix it; I couldn't make it ok for them. I could only try to make it better. I had to find a way to be useful for them to process what happened and the aftermath. This was the hardest part of the experience. Sometimes our biggest hurt is when we see our loved ones' pain. We become connected with those who are suffering – because we don't just connect through positive experiences. That is the power of love. It was heartbreaking to see my children's pain and to be powerless to stop it. I could only witness it and comfort them. But then I slowly discovered that if I modelled what life could look like, they could follow.

And they did. Because, as Daniel Siegel writes, 'Love connects us and expands who we are'.

At first, I was fearful. I felt like a balloon floating away in the air, the line which had been my connection to my identity and safety having been abruptly cut. I was treading in unfamiliar territory because everything was foreign. It felt as if I was walking on a pond covered with ice – a heavy sheet in some parts and just a thin, brittle layer in others. One misstep and I could crash through the ice to be consumed by the cold, dark water below. I conquered my fear through love. No matter where I am in the world, I am home when I reflect on the love my children and I have for each other, and how that love changes our lives and the lives of others.

The effect of our link to loved ones is confirmed by science. When there's a connection, brains tend to sync up with each other. One of the top positive psychology researchers Dr Barbara Fredrickson calls this positive resonance; it gives us a sense of intimacy and makes us feel good. She says that our way of thinking about love is limited and encourages us to expand our definition of it beyond romance to focus on *micro moments* of positive resonance that can happen in daily life to create momentary connection. It could be a deep conversation with a friend, where you become in 'tune' with each other. Your actual biochemistry syncs up, including your heartbeat and neural firing, to create a momentary resonance. This, she says, is love. Not only does it feel good and improve our social interactions, it also improves our physical health. 'Connections are biological imperatives' that are life giving to the self and others.

As is the case for many of us, loving and caring for others came easier to me than loving myself. So much so that my life is centred around the World Happiness Summit and helping others to find happiness, purpose, health and satisfaction. Helping people is a significant area where I experienced post-traumatic growth. I developed new, deeper connections, especially to those who have experienced pain. While I hope happy people become even happier, I am most motivated by helping people who are broken. We are all chipped around the edges, if not a little broken. The wonderful thing is, however, that just like the ancient Japanese art and philosophy of *kintsugi* (the Japanese art of repairing broken pottery with lacquer and gold), we can become stronger in the places where we broke. Like the gold in *kintsugi*, love can be the paste that puts us back together into a new creation. Love can help us to heal and become happier. Through pain, connection and love I became a social entrepreneur and wellbeing advocate. And I am so gratified when people share stories about how their lives were transformed by attending WOHASU.

Several people have asked me over the years, 'How were you able to go from that level of loss to dedicating your life to happiness?' I've spent a lot of time thinking about this question, especially while writing this book. The best answer that I can come up with is that my husband loved me that much. And this kind of love has filled me, even years after the lover has gone – because, as we know, love transcends time and space. Also, its foundation was a complete acceptance of who I am as a person, with full knowledge of my imperfections. He was not blind to them, which is what makes the love so powerful and lasting. He loved me because of them – because they are a part of what makes me me.

Humans have a great need for belonging. While ours was not a perfect marriage, we felt that we belonged to each other. We experienced romantic love, but our marriage was richer because there was also 'friendship love', making our relationship much more meaningful and stronger. And I still feel him cheering me on as he did when he was alive.

As we can see, love is a wonderful way to improve any kind of relationship, which is very important because our social relationships are the greatest contributor to our happiness. Dr Robert Waldinger, who spent decades on the longest scientific study on happiness, says, 'If you want to make one choice today that will make you healthier and happier – pay attention to your connections with other people'. Life is really about people, whether in a personal or professional setting.

While it can feel magical, love does not happen by magic. It requires effort, awareness and action to develop and nurture it, so that it is sustainable. This is especially true of long-term relationships or marriage. All too often, we stop seeing the other person as the gift they are to our lives, eventually focusing on the things they *don't* bring into our lives instead of purposely looking for all the good things they do for us. I wish that I could have told Ricardo more how much I appreciated all the things he did for our family and those he did specifically for me. Expressing gratitude for the 'little things' is one way that we can improve our relationships; remember, little things over time become big things. We can also choose to acknowledge what they did 'right'. For example, if your loved one goes shopping and brings nine out of the ten items on your list, don't focus on the one item they forgot. How many times do we do this in our lives? We take a deficit perspective instead of developing an abundance mindset. Perhaps just mention it and then let it go; don't get stuck on the negative.

Try also to create more opportunities to share things that you like doing together. Given that a large part of any long-term relationship is addressing financial and parenting decisions, things breaking down in the house, what's for dinner, etc., find the things that allow you to connect through positive emotions. If you feel you have forgotten what you enjoy together, schedule time without kids, work, television or phones to reconnect. Find something you both enjoy, then prioritise it and do it frequently.

For love to last, we must express it. But how? Some of the great ways are through kindness, forgiveness and gratitude. Naturally, it is easier to access these skills if we have practised building them up (we will explore these in more detail in later chapters). We can choose to invest time and energy in developing these ways of being and doing, so we build up our resilience. More than ever, we need skills that make us more resilient, and not only bounce back from life's challenges, but even grow from them. Research shows that happy people are more resilient, and we can become happier by experiencing more positive resonance and engaging in altruistic behaviour, as well as practising more gratitude and forgiveness. We become more resilient through being kind to others and ourselves. Kindness is love in action.

Love comes in many colours. Have you ever experienced a sense of awe when you were surrounded by a spectacular landscape? Or have you ever been speechless in front of a beautiful piece of art or when listening to a prayer? This is love, just of another kind. Beyond romantic, familial and community love, there are other types of love, including spiritual and the love of oneself. Through connecting with God, nature or a higher purpose, we experience spiritual love, which can give our lives a greater sense of meaning and positively impact our families and communities.

I've left love for the self until last because it was the last kind of love that I learned. I also learned that it's the most important kind, and should actually be first – because healthy love, like happiness, comes from the inside out. Perhaps that is why I was not as happy as I could have been in the past. Only now have I been able to experience the greatest happiness because I am aware of the significance and meaning of self-love, which includes self-acceptance, self-compassion, self-esteem and self-care.

It was challenging at first. As a mom and wife, I was used to placing my needs last. Sometimes I was not even aware that I had a particular need that I wasn't addressing. Our bodies may tell us first before our hearts and minds catch on. For example, when I am feeling stressed, my sleep suffers, I don't eat well and I lose weight. Because of the mind–body connection, the body is an excellent source of data, *if* we pay attention; and here, too, awareness is the first step.

As I said, for many of us the most difficult person to love is oneself. This could be as a result of shame or a lack of self-forgiveness for mistakes made in the past. Or other people might have impacted our sense of self-worth through things they did or said to us. Past relationships may have left us with open wounds that impacted our identities and self-esteem in negative ways. It is important to remedy these things because self-love is key to sustainable happiness and wellbeing. We need to develop compassion, understanding and forgiveness for what we did, did not do or failed in doing. (We will see in the next chapter how forgiveness can improve our lives in many important ways.)

Only when you accept and love yourself do you have the capacity to see all the choices you can make. It also gives you the strength and courage to make the necessary changes and decisions to get to where you want to go. Once you learn to love yourself, you also learn to appreciate, respect and take care of yourself, and you stop looking for another person to complete you. Only you can make yourself whole, and healthy self-esteem is an important pillar to build your life on. Increased self-esteem generated from self-love benefits your relationships, and improves school, work, mental health, physical health and antisocial behaviour. Please note that true self-love is not narcissism. On the contrary – it involves being kind to others, as being altruistic is another way to become happier, and happier people are more altruistic, creating a beneficial loop. During positive social encounters, we enhance our physical and emotional wellbeing thanks to the release of the hormone oxytocin, which lowers blood pressure and heart rate and reduces stress.

Through self-love I learned the importance of self-care and boundaries of love. Self-care is critical to loving yourself. It can come in many ways, including asking for what's important to you, taking time to rest and heal, prioritising your own wellbeing, checking in with your feelings, taking vacations, calling a friend, journalling, exercising, asking for help and moving away from *people pleasing* or the tendency to place others' needs before your own. While it is natural to want to help friends, family and colleagues, you must be mindful not to neglect your own needs, so that you don't become depressed, resentful or burn out. Research shows that people pleasing is rooted in a lack of a sense of self. Moving on from this may require formal therapy because its source can be in a childhood trauma. It's clear that through self-acceptance and self-love, however, we can best love others and feel the love that they have for us.

Loving others doesn't necessarily mean doing everything they ask. In fact, another way to express self-love and love for others is holding boundaries of love. Sometimes we put boundaries in place to keep ourselves healthy and safe; other times it's for their safety, particularly for children. I placed boundaries of what I allowed my children to do when they were younger, especially when I became a single parent. While it can be difficult, we might find that the most loving thing we can tell our child is 'no'. It is our duty as parents to keep our children safe. And it is the nature of our children to push the boundaries. That is ok. But it is important to learn how to say no without anger or guilt.

We all know that loving someone can involve hurt, and relationships end. They might end because our person passed away or because the relationship was not a good fit. Sometimes it is not easy to move on from a break-up because, as we have seen, the nature of our brain is to ruminate on the same thoughts, like a hamster on its wheel. For example, we may keep saying, 'Why did the person behave like this?' 'Why didn't they change?' 'Could I have done something different?' 'If they loved me enough, they would have not done this or that.' Sometimes we can't stop thinking about the person who can't love us or the person who left. In these cases, the magic word is 'yet'. 'I can't stop thinking about them *yet*.' With this small reframe, we implicitly state that it will happen at some point in time. It also helps if you avoid the triggers that take you there. For example, if checking that person's social media feed takes you back to feeling the pain of the break-up, don't do it.

While you might feel lonely when you are not in a romantic relationship, when you learn to love yourself, you become open to other meaningful and loving relationships that matter. Love can unexpectedly come into your life again, but not if you are still holding on to the past. Once you move away from the pain, disappointment and negative chatter in your brain, you create space for good things, including love. Remember that loving and accepting yourself enhances self-esteem, which also benefits relationships because you reflect on who you truly are, giving you an increased sense of belonging. How you express your love is something you can control, which is wonderful when experiencing the results of uncontrollable events in life.

TIPS

1. With your new understanding of love, identify other people you love beyond your family. How do you feel when you are with them? What qualities are enhanced in you when you spend time with them?

2. If you want to expand your social connections, join a club or class focused on something that you like to do or are interested in. You can also volunteer or go to new places and meet new people.

3. Cultivate relationships at work. Make time for people and practise active listening – meaning not just waiting for your turn to speak. Don't gossip. Set boundaries, meet commitments, and say *thank you*.

9

FORGIVENESS – IT'S A SUPERPOWER

'The weak can never forgive. Forgiveness is the attribute of the strong.'

Mahatma Gandhi

Stepping out of anger and resentment can be very hard, especially when we have been grievously wronged. Our sense of trust may have been violated when we were most vulnerable. Yet, few actions can create such a sense of relief, freedom and space for beneficial things in life as forgiveness. It makes us stronger, physically and emotionally.

But what is forgiveness, anyway?

Forgiveness is about letting go of resentment and anger towards the person or people who hurt us. Importantly, it is not about forgetting, condoning or letting the other person off the hook, but according to leading forgiveness expert Dr Fred Luskin, Director of the Stanford Forgiveness Projects, you forgive 'because it frees yourself from a prison that you have created . . . When you don't forgive everything, mind and body are disrupted. And so that's giving the offender huge power over us. Forgiveness, actually, is taking our power back and that's what people don't grasp.' Truly understand and accept this: we forgive for *ourselves*.

I have chosen to forgive people who have hurt me during several periods of my life. Consider this: the person who injured you might not even be thinking about you, may not think they harmed you, might know they hurt you and not care; or he/she might have passed away. By not forgiving, you are letting them live rent free in your brain. Ruminating about them might be clouding your decisions and your wellbeing. Plus, they could be indirectly negatively impacting the happiness of your loved ones in the present because of how the experience *continues* to impact you. If that's not a big enough reason to entertain forgiveness, I don't know what is. As Luskin says, 'forgiveness does not change the past, but it changes the present'.

There were people I didn't want to forgive because the injury was too great. I thought that if I forgave them, it would diminish what happened. However, what I found was that what actually diminished with forgiveness was the pain. But there are more benefits, including better stress management and mental health, reduced risk of all-cause mortality and less rumination. Forgiving allows us to become unstuck to the person who caused us pain or disappointment. And as with so many principles in cultivating happiness, forgiveness is well worth the effort and time well invested. The return is significant and can ripple out. It provides the healing that creates space for time to soothe our hurt. That's why it's a superpower.

The beauty of forgiveness is that in letting go of the bitterness and resentment, we receive a greater sense of peace and agency, which is wonderful because often, the injuries that we suffer leave us feeling helpless and victimised. I want to be clear that some acts are unacceptable or inexcusable. And sometimes it is helpful to focus on the pain we are feeling because it can propel us to act and put in place boundaries that keep us physically or mentally safe – for example, leaving a toxic workplace or relationship. So here, being aware of the hurt is important in taking the necessary steps to be healthy. And anger, in this case, can be very helpful because it can push us to leave an abusive relationship. The forgiveness process can only start from a position of safety.

Pain can be useful, but at some point, the healthy

decision is to let go of the past – and forgiveness helps to get us there. We can get stuck in the events that happened in our lives. But by moving away from identifying as victims, we gain power to heal and move on to the better things in life, like beauty, wonder, creativity, gratitude, compassion, positive relationships, kindness, love and, yes, happiness. We all know that we cannot change the past, but we can learn to change our reactions to what happened. Forgiveness helps to release us from the past, live better in the present and plan for a future where we get to rewrite our stories. Also, although an apology can facilitate forgiveness, it is not a prerequisite and you can reap the same benefits with or without one.

I have a long list of people who I decided to forgive, only one of whom actually ever asked for forgiveness. I've forgiven a person who I thought was my closest ally, but who hurt me deeply instead. I chose to forgive the doctors who made mistakes, including a misdiagnosis that ultimately caused the death of my husband. I chose to forgive my mother-in-law and father-in-law for not going to their son's funeral. It still hurts today as I write about it, and I don't think that I will ever understand that, but also, thankfully, I don't know how it feels to lose a son.

I choose to have compassion for them all in different ways, and that has made me happier because I am not angry at them any more. It has taken me several years and much work to reach this point, but you'd be surprised how well you can feel after you forgive. A darkness lifts from your life, increasing your sense of empowerment and contentment. I learned from Fred Luskin that forgiveness is freedom. I gained an amazing amount of energy and many opportunities came into my life. Probably, they were there all along, but I couldn't see them because my focus was on how I had been wronged and injured, and how unfair everything was. I was dwelling on how what happened was others' fault – which it was – and how badly the people in question behaved (also true). But thinking about it kept bringing anger, disappointment and resentment to the surface, making me feel worse. Then I decided to forgive. I had to try a few times before I was truly able to forgive, let go and move on. But once I'd done so, I thought, Wow. Now I get to invest this powerful energy that I had previously spent on the other person on me! And I did. I used my renewed sense of optimism, strength and vivacity to spread the global happiness movement to new regions around the world. And the people who hurt me are not living in my brain any more.

But what about when the person we need to forgive is ourselves? Well, in that case, we release the captor and the captive. Self-compassion helps. It is a challenge and I have experienced this, too. Accepting that we did the best with the information that we had at the time is difficult. I had to forgive myself for being in a long-term relationship with someone who was not good for me. I dwelled for a while on why I stayed, I felt shame and then I decided to practise empathy on myself, forgive myself and move on.

Sometimes we hurt others and feel guilty about it. Self-compassion and empathy are key here, too. Perhaps apologising to the person concerned can help to develop these valuable life skills. When we apologise, we take responsibility for the consequences of our actions. Once we reflect on the impact of our mistakes, take responsibility, then apologise for them, we are better placed to forgive others, too.

I have found that as with so many other things, we don't know how to apologise properly. A heartfelt apology has four main elements: an acknowledgment, explanation, expression of remorse and an offer to make amends. A friend of mine recently shared with me a mistake she made involving hurting another friend's feelings. She was hosting a dinner party and didn't invite someone who ended up knowing about the event and would have loved to participate. My friend acknowledged the offence – she questioned herself, 'Why did I do that?' And the honest answer was that adding another person would have meant more work for her and less comfort due to the size of the dinner table. She explained this in a phone call with her friend, expressed remorse and said that the following day she'd felt guilty and was very sorry.

She made amends by inviting her to a paella party a few days after. Her friend accepted the apology and the invitation. They are still on great terms. An apology is a great way to show others that they matter to you.

What about the right time to forgive? When is that? The timing is subjective and depends on you. You might not be ready to forgive and that is ok – but remember that the bitterness that grows because of unforgiveness can rob you of your wellbeing and make the original injury, which might have happened years before, worse. It can also negatively impact current relationships and increase feelings of depression and anxiety.

Unforgiveness constricts our choices, while forgiveness expands our opportunities. When we are stuck in unforgiveness, we lose valuable energy in thinking about the past and feel depleted, possibly worsening a situation. To me, it's a bit like when your transatlantic flight is about to land and the captain announces that you have to circle the airport. You are circling and circling, receiving scant information from the crew. You've eaten the last pretzels in your bag. You wonder and hypothesise, making up stories in your head, thinking in circles. You are so close and know that your family and friends and life are all waiting for you below. And yet, you don't land. Forgiveness releases you from this holding pattern, stops the circling and takes you home.

If you don't know how to start the forgiving process,

no problem. You can forgive in your heart or write a letter that you don't send, not even telling the person or people concerned. This way, you let go of the hurt without having to see them. You can learn; you can train for it. Therapy can also help you get there. You can try it, until you get it. The fact that you are willing to forgive means you are halfway there. When you choose to forgive and let go, you will be surprised by the gifts that you give to yourself and others. It can feel magical, wonderfully powerful.

TIPS

When you are ready, forgive. You can follow Dr Fred Luskin's recommendations (from greatergood.berkeley.edu/article/item/nine_steps_to_forgiveness/):

1. Explore your feelings about the situation and identify what was not ok about it. Tell a trusted friend. Note – this can be the hardest part because you may relive the pain.

2. Make a commitment to yourself to feel better. What can you do? Perhaps place a time limit on rumination.

3. You don't have to reconcile. 'In forgiveness you seek the peace and understanding that come from blaming people less after they offend you and taking those offenses less personally.' Accept that sometimes people's actions hurt us for reasons unrelated to us.

4. 'Get the right perspective on what is happening. Recognise that your primary distress is coming from the hurt feelings, thoughts, and physical upset you are suffering now, not from what offended you.'

5. Acknowledge that feelings come and go. 'At the moment you feel upset, practice stress management to soothe your body's fight or flight response.' You can go for a walk, meditation, a run, do yoga, journal, etc.

6. 'Give up expecting things from your life or from other people that they do not choose to give you.'

7. 'Put your energy into looking for another way to get your positive goals met than through the experience that has hurt you.' Put more energy into appreciating what you have, rather than attending to what you do not have.

8. Focus on you. 'Remember that a life well lived is your best revenge.'

9. 'Amend the way you look at your past, so you remind yourself of your heroic choice to forgive.' Gandhi was right: it takes a lot of strength to forgive.

10

LEGACY OF KINDNESS

'Relationships constitute the single most
important factor responsible for the survival of
homo sapiens.'

Dr Ellen Berscheid, social psychologist

Nothing will directly or indirectly improve your personal or professional relationships more than kindness. We can think of it as love in action. Being kind is not only a wonderful way of being and of benefit to improving our social connections, but it is also one of the greatest tools available to us for increasing our health, wellbeing and happiness. Kindness is always an option, whether we are choosing to be kind to ourselves or others. It's something we can cultivate and it's another way to ripple happiness and expand its positive by-products. It also has a looping effect, as kind people are happier, and happier people are kinder. We are actually hardwired to feel good when we do good for others. People matter.

Mattering is a key component to kindness. I learned this from Dr Isaac Prilleltensky, former Dean of the School of Education and Human Development at the University of Miami and a renowned community psychologist with expertise in mattering. He explained to me that mattering is a multidimensional construct consisting of feeling valued by and adding value to self and others. Feeling valued is a precondition for wellbeing and relates to recognition including attachment, love or belonging. Adding value is key to meaning and is about creating impact, through self-efficacy and agency.

Feeling valued can include feeling loved, but it is not necessary – it can be about being recognised by colleagues at work (because we can be recognised and not necessarily loved). And I always knew that we want to feel valued – we all want to be loved, liked or accepted. But what fascinates me and changed my perspective is that for optimal wellbeing, we need to feel that we *add* value. Often, we focus on what others can bring to us, but we have a need to contribute to others, too, thus generating value that they receive through our actions. That is very powerful because it gives us a feeling of participation, mastery and self-determination. And, when we meet that need, we feel happier. This is yet another example of the positive looping mechanism within our biology.

Mattering can also improve workplace engagement and job success, while reducing burnout. Kindness and mattering have such significant positive impacts that, according to Columbia University kindness expert Dr Kelli Harding, human-resources manuals can be reduced to two words: *be kind*.

I have found that any given situation is enhanced by being empathic, kind and treating people like they matter. While it is not always easy, it is a powerful reaction, making us feel better and reframing the situation towards positivity, allowing space for love, gratitude, forgiveness and happiness. For example, being polite to someone we don't particularly like or saying kind words to the cashier after being in a long line at the supermarket. This is not to be confused with accepting unacceptable behaviour, unpleasant situations or even agreeing with another person. As Kelli Harding says, being kind takes bravery and requires standing fearless and doesn't mean being passive or being a pushover.

It's also interesting that in business, kindness is categorised as a 'soft' skill (a non-technical skill that describes how we function and interact with people at work), as opposed to a 'hard' or technical skill. The fact that such a valuable skill is categorised in this way is remarkable because it is a purposeful and powerful reaction that has multiple positive effects on both the giver and receiver. Research on epigenetics (the study of how our behaviours and environment can cause changes that affect the way our genes work) and telomeres (parts of human cells that affect cellular ageing) is finding that loving actions can even change our physiology. For example, our brains can be changed by the secretion of feel-good hormones, and we also experience physical changes following the release of endorphins, our bodies' natural painkillers.

Importantly, being kind not only improves the quality of our lives, but also extends them, and relating to others in a positive way boosts our immune systems. Isn't this awareness amazing? Kindness can increase our sense of agency over the quality of our lives. We can do something about how we feel in our lives. We don't have to wait to see how others treat us and then react. We can be proactive in creating the lives we want.

As I said earlier, people matter, and my husband was very good at demonstrating this. Kindness was second nature to him. He was one of the most thoughtful, kind people I have ever met. I have dozens of letters that were sent to me after he passed away. He did so many things for people, helped out in so many situations, called some people who had health problems daily, others weekly. While travelling for work, he would meet strangers on aeroplanes who'd later become his close friends. He was very curious and asked many questions. Sometimes he learned that a stranger's family member was sick and because he was a doctor, he helped them in seeking better treatments. Yet he never bragged about it. Being kind came easily to him. He was happiest when he was serving, and he loved taking care of people. Ricardo was a gentleman and, as a consequence of his example, our sons are gentle men. This is what a legacy of kindness means to me, and it is one of the main reasons why I decided to make it a key pillar of WOHASU. Whenever I speak, I share the benefits of kindness and mattering; and the summit always has a section relating to this. Additionally, I try to collaborate only with people and organisations that reflect this way of being.

I have experienced the amazing benefits of acting kindly and have been a benefactor of others' kindness. Kindness is a happiness driver, and it has made a significant positive impact in my life and relationships. My sister has always been kind, but the generosity and compassion she showed me after my husband died was life giving. She slept with me in my bed for four months after his death, so that I would not be alone. Her presence helped me feel safe, valued and loved. She was a harbour to the crashing waves of my emotions. I'm grateful to my brother for making the funeral arrangements – that wasn't easy. No one ever wants to do that, and he did it with love and kindness. I felt his support giving me strength to do what I needed to do. Another powerful act of kindness came from my good friend who lost her husband the exact day a year before. She was able to step out of her own grief to visit me the day after Ricardo passed and reassured me that I would survive it and that I was going to be ok. Having people believe in you and tell you about it, especially when you are very low and struggling to see yourself in a different light, can jump-start your life.

I have also received support from partners, speakers and volunteers collaborating with me in organising the World Happiness Summit, helping with travel arrangements, sponsorships, venue selection, design or brainstorming. One year, the talented and generous chef Maria Loi closed her restaurant in Manhattan and hosted a dinner for fifty happiness experts and enthusiasts to spread our mission.

Another beautiful act of kindness I received came as a Christmas gift. I absolutely love this time of the year. Now it's bittersweet, but I treasure the nostalgic feelings I get when we choose and dress the Christmas tree as a family. In December 2022, I was working away from home, preparing for WOHASU in Italy, and got back just a few days before Christmas. On arrival, I saw that my kids had bought the tree and the lady who helps with my house decorated it, so that when I came home it felt like the holidays and family time.

The kindness that so many people have shown me over the years is impossible to list but it has made a significant impact on my success and happiness, and I appreciate it all.

Nevertheless, sometimes being kind takes effort. We might think, Why should we be gentle to the woman at the checkout if it is her job? The key to unlocking a kinder attitude and acting with kindness is empathy. It involves stepping into someone else's shoes or recognising, understanding and sharing their perspective or point of view. With the person at the checkout, we can choose to smile and say 'thank you' because maybe they're tired after a long work shift. We may never know what is going on in someone else's life, but maybe an act of kindness will make a positive difference in their day; it can make it better.

We can see how empathy helps us to be kinder and more compassionate and can support prosocial behaviour that is not forced. And empathy can be improved upon by looking for common values with other people and creating meaning out of shared experiences. We are predisposed to look for differences, but what about looking for similarities? As Dr Kim Cameron says, 'Strong positive relationships do not just occur by chance but are built on positive practices'. In other words, we can train for it.

Acting kindly to family and friends fills our hearts

and elevates our moods as our bodies release 'love' hormones and we see the reactions in our loved ones. Acting or thinking kindly in difficult situations or towards people we don't like is transcendental. We rise above the discomfort and become the best versions of ourselves. There is a certain element to kindness, as in forgiveness, that is liberating, particularly when it is hard. Being kind to someone when we are upset is difficult, so it can be helpful to take a few deep breaths to centre ourselves and diminish our fight-or-flight reaction. Sometimes saying nothing is the best thing to do. Once we are able to process our feelings around a situation, we can then evaluate the choices at our disposal. Our first reaction might be to snap at someone because we are angry, hungry or tired, but once we've practised a calming exercise (for example, taking five deep breaths), we can make a different decision. (It takes about ninety seconds for the initial stress response to fizzle out, unless we choose to prolong it through our thinking and behaviour.)

If we remind ourselves about the benefits associated with being kind, we might choose more prosocial behaviours. As we have seen, much growth can occur when engaging in positive behaviours that are challenging. We might do them because they feel good in the moment, but many times, the positive feelings come later – like a gift that was delayed and finally arrives in the post, bringing with it freedom, release and satisfaction. I have experienced this effect after responding with empathy when my kids were having a difficult time. Upon reflection, I felt pride and satisfaction in not reacting by saying something that I would regret. In short, we feel happier when we are kind.

As we explore all the ways that we can show kindness to others, let's not forget to be kind to ourselves. This is part of self-care and self-love, which we discussed in Chapter 8. Think of yourself as your best friend, or at least a very good friend. This is a tool that has served me well. When I made a mistake, I used to say to myself, 'How stupid of me' and on and on and on . . . This felt self-defeating and extended the life of a situation that could have just been a blip, but through thinking in this way, became a bigger deal than it was. Now I say, 'I made a mistake and what can I learn?' I may want to say the stupid part, but I slow down my thinking, ask the question, 'Am I stupid or did I just make an error or not have enough information?'

Few of us choose to punish our friends, but for some reason – maybe something rooted in childhood – we often feel we need to punish ourselves for our mistakes. Use the acceptance that you show to someone you care for to your own advantage, too. Use the skills you already have and internalise them when thinking of yourself: by looking at yourself through the friend lens, you will probably experience more self-compassion and it will also help you to feel better about yourself, leaving you with more energy to tackle the issue at hand. Being kind to yourself can also improve your social connections because the relationship you have with yourself is the base from which to establish healthy relationships with others.

Another significant motivator for investing in improving and expanding social connections is that kindness is an antidote to loneliness. This is incredibly important because of the negative health effects associated with loneliness and the rate at which it is growing around the world. Here, we are not talking about solitude, which can be beneficial (we all need quiet time at some point, so that we can rest). The effects of loneliness on our health can be as bad as smoking fifteen cigarettes a day, obesity or consuming too much alcohol. In fact, according to the United States Surgeon General Dr Vivek Murthy, 'human relationships are as essential to our wellbeing as food and water'.

One way that we can counteract loneliness is through kind acts. We can approach a co-worker sitting alone in the cafeteria, we can ask someone how their day is going, we can smile at a stranger and we can invite a friend who has recently experienced a loss to a movie. When I was deep in my grief and struggling with loneliness, I had friends who invited me to dinner or shopping and treated me like I was 'normal'. Loneliness carries a certain amount of stigma, so we tend to hide it. I did that. Sometimes I still do. The thing is that we can feel lonely in a room full of people – grief or depression can do that to you. All too often, we shy away from people who are going through challenging times, which makes them more lonely. Instead, we need to reach out to them, while also being kind to ourselves, remembering that it is ok to experience discomfort when we don't know what to say or how to act. Doing new things is hard, but we can learn and grow together, and here's the thing: as best-selling authors Jen Fisher and Anh Phillips say, giving and receiving help is one of the easiest and most tangible ways to build human connection. Kindness does that.

TIPS

1. Ritualise your relationships by scheduling a monthly event that gives you an opportunity to be kind. Maybe volunteer with a friend, co-worker or family member.

2. Add kindness to your family's diet. Teach it to your kids by modelling it. Smile more. Say please and thank you. Use more words like 'us' and 'we', to be more inclusive. For example, 'What do you want to do today?' becomes 'What can we all do today that is fun for all of us?' so reframing a weekend activity. Children follow your lead.

3. Practise being kind to yourself. Take a couple of minutes to say positive affirmations about you. You can say things like, 'I love you', 'I'm smart', 'I'm courageous', 'I can learn', 'I was successful before and I can do it again'. It might feel strange at first, but it can help you to become more accepting of your imperfections. We all have them. Take time to notice the good.

PART 5

ENHANCED
SPIRITUALITY

11

THE THREE MS – MEDITATION, MINDFULNESS AND MEANING

'. . . success, like happiness, cannot be pursued; it must ensue . . . as the unintended side-effect of one's personal dedication to a cause greater than oneself.'

Viktor E. Frankl, Austrian psychiatrist

Sometimes people tell me, 'I want your life' – because they see posts on social media, which I only engage in as a work necessity. They forget that the life I lead today was forged in fire. I had to walk through flames to get to the other side, and I accomplished this by making meaning out of what happened. For every genuine smile in those photos, a thousand tears were previously shed. Having said that, I am incredibly grateful that I do smile again, and I can say that I am truly happy. Still, make no mistake, it takes effort. I dedicate the first half an hour of every day, not to checking my phone for texts, news or emails, like I used to, but to reading a chapter or two from an uplifting or spiritual book that allows me to recalibrate my mood and establish the mindset that I want to foster during the day. I meditate upon my personal and professional responsibilities and aspirations, send forgiving thoughts to those who hurt me and peace to all who lack it, and pray for my children to be healthy in all ways and find fulfilment.

I am also able to be more courageous because of the meaning I get from the actions I choose to do in my life. One of the reasons I can do that is because I work on my spiritual *muscle*. For me, a spiritual life is about love, compassion and service, and about something greater than myself. The strength that I gain helps me deliver on my mission which is to help people – on a global scale – to become aware of the tools available to them to increase their happiness and wellbeing. Mindfulness is one of these important tools.

Mindfulness is a non-judgmental stance in the present moment. It is looking at an experience without attaching judgment; in other words, taking it at face value. Mindfulness also prevents time travel. We all know that we travel to the past and the future in our minds. When we are in the *here and now,* we become grounded and are less likely to ruminate over events that happened or be anxious about something happening later. How many times do we rehearse future negative conversations or situations that never happen, but in doing so, we experience them as if they have happened? By being present in the moment, we can limit that and gain a better perspective of what is actually happening. This has served me well, especially if I am afraid or anxious. By coming back to the present moment through my breath or by feeling the ground under my feet or the chair under my thighs, I can ground myself.

But there's much more. Indeed, mindfulness has many more benefits, all supported by science, including decreased anxiety and depression, minimised rumination, increased attentional skills, increased ability to manage distractions and to express oneself in various social situations and more effective emotion regulation in the brain.

During challenging times, many people around the world have started their transformation process through mindfulness meditation, which science is showing may change brain and immune function in positive ways. This is an example of the mind–body connection. The way we think and what we habitually think about impacts our bodies, both in healthy ways and in ways that cause illness. Let's remember that wellbeing is not simply the absence of illness.

Meditation, yoga and other mindfulness practices improve overall wellbeing by teaching us to be *in the moment*. We all know that spirituality means different things to different people. For me, prayer is a form of meditation, and it has enhanced my life in ways that I cannot explain except to say that it brings a stillness, clarity and peace like nothing else. Another way that I meditate is through yoga, which I practise every day. For many people, including me, meditation can be something elusive, even cryptic. That's ok. Practising yoga led me to understand that it is the nature of the mind to wander; we cannot stop it, but we can train it to come back into the now. When we engage in meditation, we are training the mind to wander less by not attaching to the thoughts that come in; instead, we can watch them float away like leaves on the surface of a gentle stream. When we are having a rush of thoughts and emotions, it is very useful to slow down our thinking or focus on something else, like our breathing, the scent of a candle or the sounds of nature. Like everything else, if you practise meditating, you become better at it, and it then becomes a tool at your disposal to help increase resilience.

A strategy that works for me is to visualise something

that I can relate to in my everyday life, like comparing life to a garden. Through our thoughts and actions, we cultivate the garden (our lives) daily. Our thoughts are the seeds, our energy is the plough and the crop is how we experience life. We can choose what we plant and take out the weeds once we see them, but to flourish, we must realise that we are the gardener.

'Hope is the number-one thing in the midst of darkness.' These are the words of Australian positive psychologist Lucy Hone, who tragically lost her young daughter in a car accident. I personally find hope in the routine investment of time that I dedicate to meditate, be mindful and focus on what gives my life meaning. This allows me to soothe my emotions and correct my thinking if needed, and happiness is a by-product of these habits. Through them, I gain the focus I need to show up in my life, which is incredibly important because it is a hopeful action that serves as a meaningful motivator. Meaning and purpose provide hope. According to Dr Michael Steger, an authority on the science of meaning, 'Meaning in life is based on feelings of significance and mattering about one's life, being able to make sense of and comprehend one's life and having purpose'. Meaning is the umbrella concept that includes purpose, a very important long-term goal that we aim to achieve but may not necessarily accomplish; the value is in its pursuit. It sits, as Steger says, in the 'future-directed, motivational realm, and is seen as the most observable and active element of meaning'.

I close my morning ritual by journalling to set my intentions. I reflect on the actions I can take that align with my values. How can my work help others? What is the best way to expand this knowledge? We all have to-do lists. What about if we decide which attitudes we want to practise each day and create a to-*be* list instead of a to-*do* list, as I mentioned earlier? We have control over that. It can look like: 'Today, I choose to be kind and helpful or courageous and curious'. These are *ways of being* that we can develop, instead of spending our day acting and reacting without enough space for awareness; without it, we miss the opportunities that we have. Once we align our actions with our values, we develop a more purposeful and meaningful life; this is spiritual to me.

As I have shared, I found my purpose after learning about the science of happiness and realising that I had become happy accidentally, but through what I later discovered were evidence-based tools. I connected with the importance of spreading this knowledge around the world. Since 2016, I have put my time, talent and treasure into organising the World Happiness Summit, and, through WOHASU, promoting approaches to improving wellbeing in all areas of life. My mission is to raise awareness that sustainable happiness is possible; that companies can transform into positive organisations; that we can go from a *me* culture to a *we* culture; and that countries can go beyond GDP (gross domestic product) as the only measure of success.

We should measure *what matters* in life and at work – because we now have enough evidence showing that happiness is beneficial in countless ways. To do that, we need universal definitions of wellbeing. Leading economists like Professor Jan-Emmanuel De Neve at the University of Oxford and Lord Richard Layard at the London School of Economics continue doing important work in this area. As Layard rightly says, 'Modern society desperately needs a concept of the common good around which to unite the efforts of its members'. To further the dialogue around country wellbeing and promote the conversation about the importance of wellbeing economics and the science of happiness, WOHASU has organised three pro bono policy meetings which we now call The World Wellbeing Policy Forum. We have hosted former heads of state of Mexico and Costa Rica, and ministers and ambassadors from several countries. This is another area of my work that I am very excited about because of the potentially meaningful impact that such meetings can have; it is truly impact at scale.

I think about how we can take WOHASU to new regions like Europe, which new training programmes we can offer, who the best speakers are for this year's summit . . . At the World Happiness Summit in Italy, we launched the Como Wellbeing Manifesto drafted by Richard Layard which called for placing wellbeing first in business and policy decisions, as well as education. These are all activities that foster my life and work purpose.

In conversation with happiness-studies expert Tal Ben-Shahar, I learned that the science of happiness provides the framework that 'strengthens our psychological immune system' and that spiritual wellbeing is an important contributor to happiness. In this sense, science becomes spiritual to me – because through this framework we are able to *feel* the science; it becomes meaningful and alive. Positive psychology acknowledges, as Dr Barbara Fredrickson says, that 'our actions and mindsets contribute a lot about how we feel in the world'. Engaging in prosocial behaviours and through growth mindsets, we can see that the principles behind sustainable-happiness approaches are self- and other-centric. In other words, it's good for us and has multiple positive impacts on others. That's why it is so important to pay attention to and cultivate it.

I am very proud of the hard work our purpose-driven team has invested in extending the ripples of happiness and supporting the evolution of WOHASU from an event to a community, educational platform and movement. I've gained a significant amount of meaning from my work. My happiness was hard fought, so I treasure it. I value it so much that I choose to take actions like forgiving people who hurt me greatly – because those actions increase my wellbeing and, in doing so, provide the pillar that helps me fulfil my life purpose. That, in turn, makes me happier.

Let's remember that happiness is not always about an elated emotional state. To me, living my purpose, experiencing flow, practising resilience, mindfulness and gratitude, being kind and useful, serving, nurturing, loving and forgiving others, plus speaking from the heart and listening, are living a *good* life. And this is what I mean by happiness.

TIPS

1. Choose a time during the day to engage in a contemplative practice like meditation, prayer, yoga or a walk in nature. Try one or two and then pick one that works for you. Remember, this can be short in duration – the important thing is to do it regularly. How do you feel after? You might want to journal some reflections.

2. Explore your life purpose by setting long-term goals that matter to you. When goal setting, keep in mind the SMART process: goals should be **s**pecific, **m**easurable, **a**ttainable, **r**elevant and **t**ime bound. Setting significant goals can help you to develop an increased sense of agency and purpose. It can also help you to gain focus and clarity and help you to act. One way to define your purpose is by connecting to your values. You can also explore what you are passionate about or how you can positively impact your community. Once you define your purpose, you can discover what matters to you the most. Write down your goals and commit to them. Visualise how you are going to pursue your future, so that you can map a course of action and use the SMART process above. Notice small gains along the way.

3. Watch my TEDx Talk 'The Bridge to Happiness' (www.youtube.com/watch?v=rcgJo9IGxx).

12

GRATITUDE

'Acknowledging the good that you already have
in your life is the foundation for all abundance.'
Eckhart Tolle, spiritual teacher

It is very difficult to be grateful and unhappy at the same time. It is as if the two cancel each other out. But it's important to note that for gratitude to be effective it must go beyond an attitude or intention, into practice. The act of being grateful is what increases our happiness. Whether you write a thank-you note or email, keep a gratitude journal or simply say thanks with a smile, that is what makes the positive change. Another added bonus of this behaviour is that when you express it to others, both parties benefit: what is good for the giver is good for the receiver. Here is another example of our looping systems at work.

Appreciating all the wonderful people, comforts and

moments in our lives is a great tool to increase our happiness when things are going well, but when the winds strike, practising gratitude can be the strong root that anchors our tree of life. 'In fact, it is precisely under crisis conditions when we have the most to gain by a grateful perspective on life,' says leading gratitude researcher Dr Robert Emmons. Intuitively, in the heartbreaking moment when doctors and nurses surrounded my husband's hospital bed trying to save his life, I used gratitude as a positive coping mechanism. I think that was the first time I became aware of, 'What can I make out of this? What's within my control?' What was happening was so foreign and playing out at such an alarming pace: one minute I was calmly speaking to the doctor in the waiting room, then his beeper alarm went off and we were running to my husband in the intensive-care unit. I thought two things at the same time: It is not possible. I refuse to step into this moment, *and*, It's happening. It's my turn to live an *unbelievable* experience. Let's go figure out how to do it.

It was chaos in the external setting – machines beeping and people coming in and out – and this matched the chaos that I was feeling inside. I felt like I would drown in a vortex of water draining down a pipe if I didn't find an anchor. And it was happening very quickly. I realised I could not stop him dying, but I needed something to hold on to, to stop me from being engulfed by the moment. I made a choice: I could be grateful for him. This is one of the first times that I remember consciously slowing down my thinking to be able to see my choices.

How I showed up at that moment was within my control. So I started saying 'thank you', over and over again. Thanking the universe, God, the world for the person who I was losing. Thanking him for being a great father and unique husband who loved me profoundly and accepted me completely. I was also grateful that he died quickly, without pain and without fear. The doctors and nurses looked at me as though I had lost my senses, but I felt a calming peace. I was acting in alignment with my values. I was also conscious that this was about him, not me – that would come later. So I decided that I would be there for him one last time. I am very proud because I did it; I showered him with love and gratitude. I am not exactly sure how it happened, but I handled that moment like a *rock star*. I am very thankful for that, and for the friends and family who were there with me then. I am most grateful that he was the father of my children because he provided a living example of how to be a kind, compassionate and generous person.

It's interesting that I didn't remember all this until my sister brought it up in conversation about five years later during a happiness training session. We were discussing gratitude and she said, 'You did that'. I think that the trauma of his death blocked the memory. We remember based on peak experiences, good or bad (see page 63), and how events end. Ricardo's death was the *mother* of bad peak experiences, and it certainly was final and impactful. For a long time, I was stuck with the dying part. But now, I focus on how amazing it is that he lived and how grateful I am that we were able to craft a life together. I've discussed this several times with my friend Mo Gawdat, former chief business officer of Google X and founder of the One Billion Happy Foundation, who, sadly, experienced the loss of his wonderful son. Yes, our loved ones pass away and that brings boundless pain, but we can decide to celebrate the fact that they lived, and that can bring gratitude and, eventually, even happiness.

I chose not to lose faith in God, love and life because I didn't get what I wanted; instead, I decided to focus on being grateful for what I still had: my kids. Even though I will never understand why Ricardo died so abruptly and so young, gratitude gave me a sense of calm in a hyper-chaotic and traumatic situation. Before there is pain, there is shock. I knew that I had to face my children and the best way for me to comfort them was by being calm. Gratitude provided space for that; I looked for reasons to be thankful when what I naturally wanted to do was say, 'Why did this happen to me?'

The one time I allowed myself to think, Why me? my mother helped me through it. She said, in a kind tone, 'Why not you?' Really, so many difficult and unfair events happen around the world; there is much suffering and catastrophes. Indeed, why not me? Life happens to everyone. There may be small challenges, medium-sized disappointments or life may fall apart in a big way. And sometimes, we must face the unimaginable. But we can use our imaginations and strengths to cope in a way that is healthier and helps us to feel better about what happened, if not in the moment, then later. Even if we are just thinking about what *could* be in the future, we are sprinkling seeds for what we may grow into later. We can do that. But we can only do it if we know that we can, and if we commit to do it. It is difficult, but for me, the alternative was impossible. I realised I could be depressed and bitter for the rest of my life and that would not bring him back. So I decided to manifest the joy, kindness and love that he brought to my family's life.

Gratitude invites happiness because it expands our perspective from the narrow, and what is immediately in front of our eyes, to the broad – what lies beyond the horizon. We can gain a bird's eye view of what we have and recognise that we actually have much more than we may previously have thought, thus creating a reframe into an abundance mindset. Through this awareness, we can think, Hey, I have a lot of things to be grateful for.

The loss also helped me to appreciate kind people who help make ordinary experiences special. We don't need to wait to be grateful for gigantic things in life; better yet, we can practise gratitude in everyday moments and, in doing so, we can potentially elevate them into special interactions. We can savour these moments, extending their length. Whether it is someone bringing you coffee, opening a door, paying you a compliment, giving you help at work, whatever – say *thank you*. It is not enough to just think about it – express it. This way we don't risk taking people for granted. Through gratitude practices we show people that we see them and that they matter to us.

In the words of Brené Brown, practising gratitude is 'how we acknowledge that there's enough and that we're enough'. It is a fundamental part of sustainable happiness – one that you can control and that you can get better at doing. Because it is learnable. According to Harvard Medical School, it is also worthwhile because in addition to increasing happiness and other positive emotions, gratitude improves health and relationships, increases resilience and helps us to savour good experiences. First thing in the morning or last thing before going to bed is best because this way you don't let other things get in the way. Maybe buy a journal that appeals to you or one featuring an inspiring message to motivate you and keep a pen or pencil with it. These recommendations may seem obvious, but the idea is to plan well, so increasing the likelihood that you will do it.

You might also want to consider a gratitude jar in which your family can post notes at random times of the day. You will be able to see the jar filling up, which is a nice experience in itself. Then decide a time and interval when you will gather to read the notes. This gratitude practice then becomes an opportunity for increased connection and relationship building.

Some people don't like to write about gratitude; it might feel forced to them. Using the camera in your phone to take photos of what you are thankful for can be a good option instead. You can then create an album in your phone and watch it grow. This is also something that you can share with friends and family. At work, you can send thank-you emails to co-workers who help you. And you can still say thank you for all the things that people are supposed to do – it's an investment in your relationships which, as we have seen, is also an investment in your happiness.

Another powerful reason to practise gratitude is that it can help us to stop ruminating because it serves as a replacement thought for what we may be dwelling on. It also resets our brains towards the positive. While we cannot will ourselves to feel grateful, be less depressed or happy, we can take positive actions. According to Robert Emmons, 'Feelings follow from the way we look at the world, thoughts we have about the way things are, the way things should be, and the distance between these two points'. When disappointment strikes, gratitude provides a perspective from which we can view life in its entirety and not be overwhelmed by temporary circumstances. Yes, this perspective is hard to achieve, but it's worth the effort because in trying, you eventually become.

I learned the hard way not to take things or people for granted. I also discovered that the life you think you will have may not turn out the way you thought. I put my energy into feeling grateful then, and this investment grew and blossomed into the resilient, multicoloured, fragrant flower that is my life today. I am so very thankful for all the support, kindness and compassion that I experienced during such a difficult time in our family's life. Being grateful has been like a healing balm on my broken heart and a big part of my happiness practice. As Emmons explains, gratitude 'is not just purely positive, but it has its power within this context of a redemptive twist on previous suffering and adversity'. So stop, notice, linger in those joyous moments we are privileged to have. Extend them by talking about them, sharing, remembering and being grateful for them. Remember that by cultivating a habit of gratitude we can become more grateful, and thus, happier.

TIPS

1. Keep a gratitude journal: find new things to be grateful for in the ordinary moments of life. For example, instead of a general 'I'm grateful for my family', look for a more specific reason why you are grateful – perhaps, 'I am grateful that my son moved his flight to stay and support me this week'.

2. Send handwritten thank-you cards to people, including friends, family and co-workers. Be specific about what you are grateful to them for.

3. Think of one thing that you are grateful about yourself as you brush your teeth.

13

THE POWER OF THE NARRATIVE AND JOURNALLING

'We become the narratives that we construct to tell our lives.'

Jerome Bruner, American psychologist

Humans are meaning-making machines. We are the stories of who we tell ourselves we are. I chose to be the hero of my story, which allowed me to become useful to my kids, family and even organise the World Happiness Summit. WOHASU has grown into a movement for positive transformation with a significant and diverse community of changemakers who want to make the world a better place. This could only happen because I created a new narrative for my life. As Dr Margarita Tarragona, a psychologist specialising in positive psychology and narrative practices, writes: 'The way in which we think and talk about our experiences can either make problems bigger or help us to contemplate new possibilities'.

As I said earlier, I was born in Nicaragua – a poor and troubled country – and I had a complicated childhood. Several events occurred that impacted my life and therefore the internal narrative that I developed as an adult. Without being aware and because of the events that I experienced, I created a victim narrative and was living my life around the things that happened to me, not consciously working towards the life I wanted. I did not know there was a choice; I thought life just happened. But as I said in Chapter 2, our brains are very efficient, and we build frames that act like filing cabinets where we store information about our environments. With so many stimuli around us, we perceive only a portion, and we perceive according to our preset frames. My filing cabinets contained a fair amount of negativity, and so I experienced my life through that mindset, so impeding my opportunities because I could not see them. My awareness of the many wonderful things happening around me was also blocked because of the blind spots I had developed. The filter through which I experienced life was faulty, and I did not know it because it was second nature.

The most amazing thing I discovered when I learned about positive psychology and the neuroplasticity of the brain is that we can change our mindsets, and therefore change and improve our lives. It requires awareness and action. We become aware by learning and exploring; this is where my character strengths, curiosity and love of learning were useful. Because the pain of the loss was too great, I had to act. I had to move. Pain is a great catalyst for change. If you keep your hand on the stove, it burns and causes acute pain, making you move your hand to 'safe'. It is a useful natural reaction.

By becoming aware of our internal conversations, we are able to slow down our thinking and understand what messages we are telling ourselves. We can select which stories to focus on. These messages become part of our identities. Some are true, and others are not; the latter becoming true through our actions. Imagine a child is bumping into furniture as they run around the house, and they accidentally break a vase. An adult may scold them angrily and say, 'You are always so clumsy!' Perhaps the child grows up believing: 'I am clumsy', instead of, 'I ran around the house, I broke something and learned to take my time'. Then, as an adult, they have an internal dialogue that says, 'I don't do sports because I am clumsy'. We can see how this story develops into a limiting belief that negatively impacts someone's life and diminishes their opportunities.

Because of our mindsets, we are blind to our limiting

beliefs, but once we become aware of them, we can use storytelling to change our lives. According to Tarragona, 'If difficulties are seen as certain kinds of stories, solutions can be found in the authoring of different, alternative stories'.

In one moment, after a twenty-one-year relationship, I was suddenly single, with a new identity: widow. What is that? The word was so foreign and the meaning I had attached to it came from movies I had seen. For some reason, the first image that came to mind were the widows from the *Godfather* movies. A young woman, old in an instant, wearing black, never to smile again and dead inside. I saw myself going into that story and I pulled the handbrake on that ride. My internal dialogue sounded like this: 'No way. I don't know how, but this is not going to be my life. I will be happy again and I will triumph. I will become the hero of my life, not a victim of circumstance. I will wear red.'

How does one become a hero? In my case, I first decided that I would be it and then decided where I wanted to go: I wanted happiness. I then became aware that my quest would require action. I didn't realise how much action it would take, but I also didn't know that in doing, I would become. I had to act and conquer the fear of 'failure'. I have come to understand that failure is really learning. There is no rehearsal for life. It's like playing a violin concerto live in front of an audience, when you have never studied that instrument. We learn as we go along, and many times, we do not get it right on the first try. And the wonderful thing is that you can minimise the failure narrative by reframing the experience into learning. The important thing is not to keep making the same mistakes repeatedly.

When I decided to get my MBA at Georgetown, I had no idea what I was going to do with the new degree. I saw the process as an opportunity to find out what I *could* do and to connect with a new community who could perhaps open new personal and professional opportunities. As my kids did immediately after Ricardo's death, my Georgetown community saved my life. They welcomed me with open arms and supported me in ways that I can never fully explain. My new friends made space for me and respected the experience that I'd had just four months prior. One friend organised a fancy dinner at a popular restaurant for my birthday. About thirty people came to celebrate me; they even had a menu printed with my name (I still have this). The business school sent flowers to my house in Miami on the first anniversary of my husband's passing. These are impactful moments of kindness that I will never forget.

While I was pursuing my MBA, I was slowly evolving into someone new. My internal dialogue was changing. I began to feel alive and see a future which was not bleak and scary. I started asking the question:

What do happy people do? I discovered that some of the characteristics of happy people are that they get out of bed, get dressed, say yes to fun activities and exercise and have a positive outlook on the future. I started copying that; I noticed that I was becoming through the choices I was making. My internal dialogue was evolving into: 'Yes, I can'.

I want to stress here that this was not toxic positivity (pretending to be happy when you are not). I was still hurt, sad and very vulnerable, but I was also focusing on what I could control out of the experience and giving myself permission to hope, plan and flourish. I opened a window to possibilities through my pain. Notice, the window did not open – I opened it. It was challenging because I had to learn something new very quickly: how to feel whole after being married for half my life and how to feel ok being alone. And the hardest part was how to become happy while being lost and broken. I needed to do this for my kids because it was the best way I knew to provide a way out for them. It had to be through my example. I wanted them to be ok and happy, and for that to happen I had to model it for them. This, too, was very challenging.

By choosing the meaning we attach to experiences, we can create narratives that increase our sense of life purpose. As I shared previously, I decided to create meaning out of our family's painful experience. I wanted to carry Ricardo's legacy of kindness, compassion, excellence, generosity and laughter. This has left me with a feeling of expansion, including hope and letting go of the fear narrative, which is constricting and limits the possibilities for greater happiness.

Once we decide to change our mindsets to shift our narratives, it is important to find evidence that supports our new vision. We find this evidence in our strengths. We saw earlier that we can develop awareness to find what we are good at. We can then see how these strengths can contribute to our new stories and become part of our new identities. I am a very good communicator and a storyteller by nature. In fact, my first master's degree is in communication. I believe that I learned this from my father. I loved his stories. They always fuelled my imagination as a child. Perhaps my vision for the future comes from those childhood dreams.

After finishing the MBA programme, it was natural for me to take a job at a communications firm. Part of my narrative was: I am a communicator with a communications degree, so I will work in communications. While I was very good at international crisis communication management, this career did not provide what I needed to meet the new definition of success for me: purpose and meaning. I had not survived Ricardo's death and the aftermath to take a job where I did not feel fully alive. I felt that a piece was missing inside me and only significance would fill it. When I learned that there was a science behind wellbeing and evidence-based frameworks to become happier, I quit my secure job and decided to go all in on happiness.

My new narrative became: 'I am a person who chose happiness despite pain, and through conscious work, I became happy. I found boundless meaning in creating and promoting a platform for the evolving science.' This is who I wanted to be and what I wanted to do. I had no idea if I was going to be successful, but I had learned to be happy and I wanted others to have this choice and knowledge. I became a social entrepreneur, grew an event into a platform and a movement, which is alive with the principles that my husband demonstrated through his life. I feel such gratitude to learn from amazing experts, connect with a global community and share my story of growth and service. I am most happy when I can contribute to someone else's happiness. There is nothing better for me than inviting someone to a new understanding of what is possible in their lives. Again, it requires time and effort, but it's well worth it. We forget that the consequences of unhappiness can be even more time-consuming. I would rather work on ways that I can be effective and positive while taking note of challenges I need to address. Before I changed my story, I would only focus on the challenges. I have since altered my focus, and whatever I pay most attention to grows.

This does not mean I neglect my responsibilities. In fact, I have never worked so hard in my life. WOHASU keeps growing and evolving. We now offer Chief Happiness Officer and an Elements of Wellbeing certifications. I am invited to speak and share my experience around the world. In March 2023, we had our first summit outside the United States; it was in Italy, meaning that we were working within a different culture, different language and different continent. Someone recently commented that I was brave to have the World Happiness Summit in Europe. But it felt natural to me to expand the ripples of happiness to another region because I firmly believe that if we can raise people's happiness levels, we co-create a world that is healthier and more sustainable.

If you are feeling like you do not know how to become happy again or truly happy for the first time, remember to add the word 'yet' to the end of a sentence and to your internal dialogue (I could do it, so you can, too): perhaps you have not found love *yet*, or have not found life meaning *yet* or your relationship with your kids is not great *yet*. I love this word. It is just a few letters, but they convey such a powerful message of hope. And we can all use more hope.

The principles behind happiness are simple but can be hard to implement. Some days it takes more effort to reframe, while on other days it comes more easily. But for me, the price of self-pity and victimhood is very high. Certainly, following some traumatic experiences it is natural to feel like a victim and adopt that mentality. But at some point, and only you know when that is for you, it is helpful to move away from that.

There are so many things I don't know how to do . . . *yet*. But I've learned that if something is worthwhile pursuing, we need to do it. Reframing our internal dialogue is a great tool and motivator. I *will* find a way to work in Europe, while residing in Miami. I *will* find a way to finish a book with a looming deadline. We all have untapped potential, and we can adapt in positive ways by learning and acting, creating positive habits for change.

Our growth becomes part of our stories. With every small gain or step forward, we can add a bit to the hero narrative. But we can only do this if we are aware of our wins, however trivial we might think they are. Because they might seem trivial, but they bring big results.

Another thing that I've learned is to go where I am wanted. Instead of forcing situations, I have found that I want to be with people and organisations that are authentically aligned to my values and mission. Because together, we can draft stories that support each other and make our journeys much more enjoyable and productive. So while I might experience temporary disappointment about not being included, I can reframe and focus on all the times I have been invited by amazing people to do amazing things. 'I was not invited' can be rewritten: 'I am wanted'.

I carry notes in my backpack that I take wherever I travel. These are love notes friends have written to me over the years. They don't know I carry them, but they are my companions when I am away from home. I am comforted by their uplifting words – words that have helped me to grow.

I am also very grateful that my sons and I do not receive pity because this confirms the hero story. There are no victims in my family. I am gratified by how we took an unfair, painful experience and turned it around to offer people hope. The theme of my narrative is really one of hope. And my story can be reduced to four words: she grew cultivating happiness. I found a way to become happier. And you can, too.

TIPS

1. Keep notes and cards that people wrote to you complimenting or thanking you. Keep them handy so that you can reread and savour them. For example, you might want to keep one on your night table or create a digital archive of supportive emails or texts that you've received. Take a screenshot of them and create an album called 'Nice things people say to me' on your phone. Look at these from time to time. More people like us more than we think and they say nice things to us.

2. What's your self-talk? Notice which words you repeatedly think about or use when you describe yourself to yourself and others. Which words stick out? Is there a theme? Change your inner dialogue and change your narrative. Continue with the exercise below.

3. Explore how the stories you tell yourself about yourself can change the way you think about your identity. Based on Margarita Tarragona's work on the science of storytelling, you can use narratives in movies or music to help with this. See the original version of a movie or listen to the original version of a song, then compare them to remakes. How do they differ? Which do you prefer? What do you like and why? Evaluating in this way, you can also make choices about ways of being that create different versions of you, depending on which you choose to express. Invest in learning about and cultivating the new versions of you. Note: this requires creating habits, setting up rituals and reminders that you repeat regularly, transforming the idea from an intellectual concept into an experience.

AFTERWORD – BE AN ACTIVE PARTICIPANT IN YOUR LIFE; DON'T LET LIFE JUST HAPPEN TO YOU

'Being deeply loved by someone gives you strength, while loving someone deeply gives you courage.'

Lao Tzu, Chinese philosopher

After seeing Steven Spielberg's *Jaws*, I became terrified of the ocean. This deep-seated fear always bothered me because as children, my cousins and friends all enjoyed the water so much, and while I pretended it was fun, inside I was frantic with fear. My mother, who cautioned against me seeing the film, is a water animal; she passionately loves the ocean. She enrolled me in sailing classes when I was twelve years old and it was agony. Again, my peers were loving it and I was counting the minutes for class to be over. I could appreciate how beautiful the scenery was, yet my mind kept ruminating over all the things that could go wrong. In retrospect, this phobia encompassed other more real fears for my safety and security, as these needs were not met during my childhood.

In learning about positive psychology and, in particular, the concept of the growth mindset, coupled with the benefits of changing my mind frame, I decided to tackle this fear. During the lockdown resulting from the COVID pandemic, I focused on using my strengths to tackle this. I decided to use a particular strength of mine, which is a love of learning to address the fear. I enrolled in sailing lessons and learned to sail a small catamaran. I enjoyed the wind and water splashing on my face, the breathtaking beauty of the scenery and the empowerment I gained. I swam with dolphins and enjoyed the company of my fellow sailors. I conquered my fear and that made me feel more courageous in other areas of life, too.

During the pandemic, like many people, I reflected deeper on my life purpose. At first, I thought, How unlucky I am to have lived during this time in history. It felt like the end of the world, and the lockdown had significant effects on WOHASU because in March 2020 we had to cancel the summit, just six days before opening day. Then I reframed to a different and more useful thought: How fortunate I am that I get to live during a time when my work will be so useful to people. What a privilege. I was able to do that because I'd spent years learning about the principles I've shared in this book and, most importantly, because I continuously train for it through daily action. You might think that's a lot of time invested in reworking my thinking. But the alternative is not living life to the fullest, not being the best version of myself, not being present to all the beauty that is in front of my eyes. Been there and done all that – no thank you.

So I used the lockdown as an opportunity to find new ways to grow from what was happening. I chose to reflect and evaluate areas of my life where I still needed to evolve, where I was passive in accepting things that didn't fit with how I wanted my life to be and weren't aligned with my core values. I made many significant changes during this time. I ended a long-term relationship, I moved, I started jotting down ideas for this book, I reorganised my company and I learned to sail. I gained deeper resilience as part of the growth from life's latest challenges. I decided to use my life experience and knowledge of this science to serve those in need. I activated our expert network and produced and hosted forty free master classes during 2020 to help our community and public-school teachers and students. I provided pro bono happiness seminars for Georgetown Business School students, faculty and alumni. I moved our in-person Chief Happiness Officer (CHO) certification online. Then, after two years away, we organised the most successful WOHASU we'd ever had and, thanks to the suggestion of two Italians, Alberto Nobis, former CEO of DHL Express Europe and Professor Sandro Formica, we held the World Happiness Summit in Lake Como, Italy in March 2023.

Still, life brings difficult moments and then I give myself 'permission to be human', as Tal Ben-Shahar says. I feel empathy and compassion for others who have lost a loved one. I am triggered by the pandemic because my husband died of pneumonia, brought on by the flu, which is very similar to what many families went through. But I accept this, *and* I purposely look for 'silver linings' and glimmers of hope. I experience flow in my writing, ideation and creativity; I am grateful for that. I am also happy about spending more time with my sons; they are my biggest supporters. And I continue to enjoy developing platforms to help people, brainstorming with experts, meeting many wonderful people, learning about a new culture, living in different cities and searching for how I can best serve.

I chose long ago that I was going to be happy, so I continuously tap into purpose and meaning which are the well of my happiness. Through awareness, connection and experience, I use the evidence-based tools I've discussed in this book to buttress my sense of loss or anxiety when they surface, and this leads me closer to the next positive emotion. By repeatedly using these skills, they have become a natural part of my life. And when life happens, I don't have to fall as low or stay down as long because I have a framework to tap into. So yes, life is challenging, even very challenging at times, but it is also filled with electric or peaceful moments that are missed if we are not present.

I am a work in progress. I choose to savour everyday moments, and in doing so, I have found that they can become extraordinary, elevating my mood. I forgive the hurts of the past and they hurt me less. The *reality* of the situations may not have changed, but I have changed how I see my circumstances by reframing and changing my expectation of what should be. Remember, this is not a dress rehearsal; this is life. We can change. In fact, we are changing all the time. But we can change on purpose and with a direction towards something positive, and even to happiness. My kids needed me, so I chose happiness. Love broke my heart and love saved my life. By making a choice, I changed my mindset, and then I changed my life and learned to swim a new way. In doing so, I've accomplished a small part in changing the world. You too can choose happiness and change the world in your own special way.

TIPS

There are many experts, books, and courses on happiness. The best one is the one that works for you. The key is to understand that happiness is an internal process that takes daily action.

1. Create a method of working on your happiness. Remember that the principles are simple but can be difficult to implement.

2. Commit to making your wellbeing a priority every day.

3. Stick to a method long enough to give it a chance (perhaps three weeks).

4. Evaluate, continue or pivot.

5. Once you have a method, identify one area of wellbeing you want to start working on.

ENDNOTES

Shakespeare's 18th sonnet at the beginning of this book is my favourite poem. Early in our relationship, Ricardo gave me a rare edition of a book with this poem, in which Shakespeare honours his beloved and says, 'So long as men can breathe, or eyes can see, so long lives this, and this gives life to thee'. In writing the sonnet, he eternalised this special person. Through my work with WOHASU and the World Happiness Summit, I keep Ricardo's memory alive because he is the reason why I decided to dedicate my life to promoting happiness as a choice. This gives life to him, and his 'eternal summer shall not fade, nor lose possession of that fair [he] ow'st, nor shall death brag [he] wander'st in his shade . . .'

INTRODUCTION

Richard G. Tedeschi, Jane Shakespeare-Finch, Kanako Taku and
    Lawrence G. Calhoun, *Posttraumatic Growth: Theory, Research, and
    Applications*, Routledge, 2018.

CHAPTER 1

Julia K. Boehm, Peter Ruberton, and Sonja Lyubomirsky, 'The Promise of Fostering Greater Happiness', *The Oxford Handbook of Positive Psychology*, 3rd edition, edited by C. R. Snyder, Shane J. Lopez, Lisa M. Edwards and Susana C. Marques.

CHAPTER 2

E. Diener (2000), 'Subjective well-being: The science of happiness and a proposal for a national index', *American Psychologist*, 55(1), 34–43; https://doi.org/10.1037/0003-066X.55.1.34

Martin E. P. Seligman, *Flourish: A Visionary New Understanding of Happiness and Well-being*, Nicholas Brealey Publishing, 2011.

D. Kahneman and A. Tversky (1984), 'Choices, values, and frames', *American Psychologist*, 39(4), 341–350; https://doi.org/10.1037/0003-066x.39.4.341.

P. Brickman, D. Coates and R. Janoff-Bulman (1978), 'Lottery winners and accident victims: Is happiness relative?' *Journal of Personality and Social Psychology*, 36(8), 917–27.

CHAPTER 3

https:// www.britannica.com/list/nelson-mandela-quotes
https://assets.csom.umn.edu/assets/71516.pdf
Viktor E. Frankl, *Man's Search for Meaning*, Beacon Press, 2006.
Edwin A. Locke and Gary P. Latham, *A Theory of Goal Setting & Task Performance*, Pearson College Division, 1990.
E. A. Hoge, M. M. Chen, E. Orr, C. A. Metcalf, L. E. Fischer, M. H. Pollack, I. de Vivo and N. M. Simon (2013), 'Loving-Kindness Meditation practice associated with longer telomeres in women', *Brain, Behavior, and Immunity*, 32, 159–63; doi: 10.1016/j.bbi.2013.04.005. Epub 2013 Apr 19. PMID: 23602876.

Carol S. Dweck, PhD, *Mindset: The New Psychology of Success*, Random House Publishing Group (reprint edition), 2007.

M. Puderbaugh and P. D. Emmady, 'Neuroplasticity' [Updated 2022 May 8], in: *StatPearls* [Internet], Treasure Island (FL): StatPearls Publishing; available from: https://www.ncbi.nlm.nih.gov/books/NBK557811/

CHAPTER 4

https://tnhaudio.org/2014/04/15/way/

https://www.utoledo.edu/studentaffairs/counseling/anxietytoolbox/breathingandrelaxation.html

https://www.sciencedirect.com/science/article/abs/pii/S1744388121000141

https://www.betterup.com/blog/distress-vs-eustress

https://hbr.org/2015/09/stress-can-be-a-good-thing-if-you-know-how-to-use-it

https://hbr.org/2016/07/the-data-driven-case-for-vacation

Bruce W. Smith, C. Graham Ford, Kelly Erickson and Anne Guzman (2020), 'The Effects of a Character Strength Focused Positive Psychology Course on Undergraduate Happiness and Well-Being', *Journal of Happiness Studies*, 22, 343–62.

A. Linley, *Average to A+: Realising Strengths in Yourself and Others*, CAPP Press, 2008.

L. A. King and J. Trent, J., 'Personality strengths' in *Handbook of psychology: Personality and social psychology*, H. Tennen, J. Suls and I. B. Weiner (eds), John Wiley & Sons, 2012.

T. D. Hodges and J. Asplund, 'Strengths development in the workplace' in *Oxford Handbook of Positive Psychology and Work*, P. A. Linley, S. Harrington and N. Garcea (eds), Oxford University Press, 2010.

Mihaly Csikszentmihalyi, *Flow: The Psychology of Optimal Experience*, Harper Perennial Modern Classics, 2008.

CHAPTER 5

J. Thompson Coon, K. Boddy, K. Stein, R. Whear, J. Barton and M. H. Depledge (2011), 'Does Participating in Physical Activity in Outdoor Natural Environments Have a Greater Effect on Physical and Mental Wellbeing than Physical Activity Indoors? A Systematic Review', *Environmental Science & Technology*, 45(5), 1761–72.

https://www.cdc.gov/physicalactivity/basics/pa-health/index.htm

D. Kahneman and A. Tversky (1999), 'Evaluation by moments: Past and future' in *Choices, Values, and Frames*, D. Kahneman and A. Tversky (eds), Cambridge University Press.

CHAPTER 6

B. L. Fredrickson (2000), 'Cultivating positive emotions to optimize health and wellbeing', *Prevention & Treatment*, 3(0001a), 1–25.

https://hbr.org/2013/11/emotional-agility

Carol S. Dweck PhD, *Mindset: The New Psychology of Success*, Random House Publishing Group (reprint edition), 2007.

Susan David, 'The Gift and Power of Emotional Courage' (TED talk, 2018), https://www.youtube.com/watch?v=NDQ 1Mi5I4rg

CHAPTER 7

https://www.goodreads.com/quotes/791092-there-is-a-great-beauty-in-little-thing

Lisa Wood, Karen Martin, Hayley Christian, Andrea Nathan, Claire Lauritsen, Steve Houghton, Ichiro Kawachi, Sandra McCune (2015), 'The Pet Factor – Companion Animals as a Conduit for Getting to Know People, Friendship Formation and Social Support', *PLOS ONE*, 10(4): e0122085.

·Meik Wiking, *The Art of Making Memories: How to Create and Remember Happy Moments* (The Happiness Institute Series), William Morrow, 2019 (illustrated edition).

Lam Thi Mai Huynh, Alexandros Gasparatos, Jie Su, Rodolfo Dam Lam, Ezekiel I. Grant and Kensuke Fukushi (2022), 'Linking the nonmaterial dimensions of human-nature relations and human well-being through cultural ecosystem services', *Science Advances*, 8(31).

M. P. White, I. Alcock, J. Grellier, et al. (2019), 'Spending at least 120 minutes a week in nature is associated with good health and wellbeing', *Scientific Reports*, 9, 7730.

https://www.health.harvard.edu/blog/why-is-music-good-for-the-brain-2020100721062

https://www.hopkinsmedicine.org/health/wellness-and-prevention/keep-your-brain-young-with-music

S. Lyubomirsky, L. King, L. and E. Diener, E. (2005), 'The Benefits of Frequent Positive Affect: Does Happiness Lead to Success?' *Psychological Bulletin*, 131(6), 803–55.

Michelle N. Shiota (2021), 'Awe, wonder, and the human mind', Michelle N. Shiota; https://doi.org/10.1111/nyas.14588

Mayo Clinic Staff, https://www.mayoclinic.org/healthy-lifestyle/stress-management/in-depth/stress-relief/art-20044456

F. Marmolejo-Ramos, A. Murata, K. Sasaki, et al. (2020), 'Your face and moves seem happier when I smile: Facial action influences the perception of emotional faces and biological motion stimuli', *Journal of Experimental Psychology*, 67(1),14–22; doi:10.1027/1618-3169/a000470

https://hechingerreport.org/want-resilient-and-well-adjusted-kids-let-them-play/

https://www.nifplay.org/what-is-play/biological-drive-to-play/#evolved

https://www.helpguide.org/articles/mental-health/benefits-of-play-for-adults.htm

M. Clapp, N. Aurora, L. Herrera, M. Bhatia, E. Wilen and S. Wake-field (2017), 'Gut microbiota's effect on mental health: The gut-brain axis'; doi: 10.4081/cp.2017.987. PMID: 29071061; PMCID: PMC5641835

R. Mujcic and A. J. Oswald (2016), 'Evolution of Well-Being and Happiness After Increases in Consumption of Fruit and Vegetables', *American Journal of Public Health*, 106(8), 1504–10; doi: 10.2105/AJPH.2016.303260. PMID: 27400354; PMCID: PMC4940663

R. I. M. Dunbar (2017), 'Breaking Bread: the Functions of Social Eating', *Adaptive Human Behavior and Physiology*, 3(3), 198–211; doi: 10.1007/s40750-017-0061-4. Epub 2017 Mar 11. PMID: 32025474; PMCID: PMC6979515

Cassie Holmes, *Happier Hour: How to Beat Distraction, Expand Your Time, and Focus on What Matters*, Simon & Schuster, 2022.

CHAPTER 8

bell hooks, *All About Love: New Visions*, William Morrow Paperbacks, 2016.

Daniel J. Siegel, *Aware: The Science and Practice of Presence*, Tarcher-Perigee, 2018.

Barbara L. Fredrickson, PhD *Love 2.0: Creating Happiness and Health in Moments of Connection*, Plume (reprint edition), 2013.

'Remaking love: Barbara Fredrickson at TEDxLowerEastSide' (2014), https://www.youtube.com/watch?v=fHoEWUTYnSo

Robert Waldinger, 'The Secret to a Happy Life – Lessons from 8 Decades of Research' (TED talk, 2023), https://www.youtube.com/watch?v=IStsehNAOL8

Karen Reivich and Andrew Shatte, PhD, *The Resilience Factor: 7 Keys to Finding Your Inner Strength and Overcoming Life's Hurdles*, Broadway Books, 2003.

U. Orth and R. W. Robins (2022), 'Is high self-esteem beneficial? Revisiting a classic question', *American Psychologist*, 77(1), 5–17.

Scott Barry Kaufman and Emanuel Jauk (2020), 'Healthy Selfishness and Pathological Altruism: Measuring Two Paradoxical Forms of Selfishness', *Frontiers in Psychology*; https://doi.org/10.3389/fpsyg.2020.01006

CHAPTER 9

https://www.socratic-method.com/quote-meanings/mahatma-gandhi-the-weak-can-never-forgive-forgiveness-is-the-attribute-of-the-strong

https://www.mayoclinic.org/healthy-lifestyle/adult-health/in-depth/forgiveness/art-20047692.

https://www.curablehealth.com/podcast/forgiveness-is-not-what-you-think-it-is-dr-fred-luskin

Dr Fred Luskin, *Forgive for Good: A Proven Prescription for Health and Happiness*, HarperOne (reprint edition), 2003.

Loren L. Toussaint, PhD, Grant S. Shields, MA, George M. Slavich, PhD. (2016), 'Forgiveness, Stress, and Health: a 5-Week Dynamic Parallel Process Study', *Annals of Behavioral Medicine*, 50(5), 727–35.

https://www.health.harvard.edu/blog/the-art-of-a-heartfelt-apology-2021041322366

CHAPTER 10

https://www.pursuit-of-happiness.org/relationships-one-of-seven-habits-to-cultivate-happiness

Dr Martin Seligman, *Flourish: A Visionary New Understanding of Happiness and Well-being*, Atria (reprint edition), 2012.

Isaac and Ora Prilleltensky, *How People Matter*, Cambridge University Press, 2021.

Dr Kelli Harding, *The Rabbit Effect: Live Longer, Happier, and Healthier with the Groundbreaking Science of Kindness*, Atria (reprint edition) 2020.

https://www.cdc.gov/genomics/disease/epigenetics.htm

E. Sahin and R. A. DePinho (2010), 'Linking functional decline of telomeres, mitochondria and stem cells during ageing', *Nature*, 464, 520–8.

https://www.psychologytoday.com/us/basics/empathy

Kim S. Cameron, *Practicing Positive Leadership: Tools and Techniques That Create Extraordinary Results*, Berrett-Koehler Publishers, 2013.

https://www.healthdirect.gov.au/acts-of-kindness-and-compassion

J. Holt-Lunstad, T. B. Smith, M. Baker, T. Harris and D. Stephenson (2015), 'Loneliness and social isolation as risk factors for mortality: a meta-analytic review', *Perspectives on Psychological Science*, 10(2), 227–37; doi: 10.1177/1745691614568352. PMID: 25910392

Vivek H. Murthy MD, *Together: The Healing Power of Human Connection in a Sometimes Lonely World*, Harper Wave, 2020.

Jen Fisher and Anh Phillips, *Work Better Together: How to Cultivate Strong Relationships to Maximize Well-Being and Boost Bottom Lines*, McGraw Hill, 2021.

CHAPTER 11

S. L. Keng, M. J. Smoski and C. J. Robins (2011), 'Effects of mindfulness on psychological health: a review of empirical studies', *Clinical Psychology Review*, 31(6), 1041–56; doi: 10.1016/j.cpr.2011.04.006. Epub 2011 May 13. PMID: 21802619; PMCID: PMC3679190

R. J. Davidson, J. Kabat-Zinn, J. Schumacher, M. Rosenkranz, D. Muller, S. F. Santorelli, F. Urbanowski, A. Harrington, K. Bonus, J. F. Sheridan (2003), 'Alterations in brain and immune function produced by mindfulness meditation', *Psychosomatic Medicine*, 65(4), 564–70; doi: 10.1097/01.psy.0000077505.67574.e3. PMID: 12883106

Lucy Hone, 'The Three Secrets of Resilient People' (TED talk, 2019), https://www.youtube.com/watch?v=NWH8N-BvhAw

https://psychwire.com/ask/topics/16daks/ask-michael-steger-about-meaning-and-purpose-in-life

Richard Layard, *Happiness: Lessons From a New Science*, Penguin Random House, 2006.

'Remaking love: Barbara Fredrickson at TEDxLowerEastSide' (2014), https://www.youtube.com/watch?v=fHoEWUTYnSo

CHAPTER 12

Robert A. Emmons, *Gratitude Works! A 21-Day Program for Creating Emotional Prosperity*, Jossey-Bass, 2013.

B. L. Fredrickson and D. Kahneman (1993), 'Duration neglect in retrospective evaluations of affective episodes', *Journal of Personality and Social Psychology*, 65(1), 45-55; doi: 10.1037//0022-3514.65.1.45. PMID: 8355141

Brené Brown, *Daring Greatly: How the Courage to Be Vulnerable Transforms the Way We Live, Love, Parent, and Lead*, Brené Brown, Avery (reprint edition), 2015.

https://www.health.harvard.edu/healthbeat/giving-thanks-can-make-you-happier

https://greatergood.berkeley.edu/article/item/how_gratitude_can_help_you_through_hard_times

https://www.health.harvard.edu/healthbeat/giving-thanks-can-make-you-happier

https://www.happify.com/hd/the-science-behind-gratitude/

CHAPTER 13

Dr Margarita Tarragona, *Positive Identities: Narrative Practices and Positive Psychology* (in 'The Positive Psychology Workbook Series'), CreateSpace Independent Publishing Platform, 2013.

Dr Margarita Tarragona, 'Postmodern/Post-Structuralist Therapies' in *Twenty-first Century Psychotherapies*, Jay Lebow, John Wiley & Sons, 2008.

ACKNOWLEDGEMENTS AND GRATITUDE

The book-writing marathon . . . I wrote the outline for my book during the COVID lockdown and completed the book itself in a month, two years later. While on a planning trip for WOHASU in November 2022, I met with the amazing team at Rizzoli in Milan, and they saw my vision and the importance of spreading my story. They were not only interested but acted, and asked if I could finish the book by the end of December. I said yes. I am very grateful to them for believing in me and helping me to extend the ripples of happiness. I could not have done this without the support of my children, Stefan and Kristof. I not only love them, but admire them for their kindness, generosity and strength. And they now work with me, which is a dream come true. I am also very grateful for my WOHASU team, who not only cheered me on but took on extra responsibilities during that December, so that I could finish my book. Importantly, I had the good fortune to work with Cristina Sarto, a talented journalist, who was my sounding board through the book-writing marathon. She made it fun. And to the folks at the World Wellbeing Movement who hosted me at Oxford and allowed me to write in their beautiful snow-covered library – you made me feel so very welcome, thank you.

I would like to thank the wonderful Ebury team, especially my editor Holly Whitaker and my copyeditor Anne Newman for enhancing the English edition. I'm very grateful.

I have had the privilege to have learned and continue to learn from the amazing minds researching, studying, practising and advocating for happiness and wellbeing methods. Some of these brilliant people who have joined me at the World Happiness Summit are Richard Layard, Sonja Lyubomirski, Tal Ben-Shahar, Mo Gawdat, Margarita Tarragona, Sandro Formica, Jen Fisher, Jan-Emmanuel De Neve, Alberto Nobis, Maria Sirois, Itai Ivtzan, Isaac Prilleltensky, Robert Biswas-Diener, Kelli Harding, Maria Loi, Fred Luskin, Martin Seligman, Laurie Santos, Alla Klymenko – and there are many more.

I am also incredibly grateful to my sister, Tessy, not only for being there for me throughout this journey, through thick and thin, but also for the joy that is her presence. My brother, Jurgen, helped me when I needed his support with WOHASU, and I am very grateful. Thank you to my parents, Jurgen and Karen, and my sister-in-law, Inge, for supporting me.

This book is dedicated to the love I have for Stefan,

Kristof and Ricardo. This love made happiness a possibility.

Studying happiness is not only a worthy pursuit, but researching, reading, writing and discussing it make the participant happier. You may want to try it.

MORE THINGS I DO TO CULTIVATE MY HAPPINESS (IN NO PARTICULAR ORDER):

- A very cold shower to reset; it's invigorating, especially if I'm in a funk. It literally helps me to 'snap out of it'.

- I don't sleep with my phone. I don't check it after 9pm or during the first half hour I'm awake in the morning. Our brains are very susceptible right before sleep and when we've just woken up. So I try to take care of my brain. I've found that I ruminate less while trying to sleep and this has helped me feel more rested.

- And speaking of sleep. When I wake up tired, I explore what my body is trying to tell me. Then I take action. And I also nap. I cannot overstate the value of rest. It also makes me so much more productive and creative.

- I slow down my thinking. What can I control in this situation? Which action serves me or others best?

- When I don't exercise, I feel terrible! Every day I do ten minutes of yoga and light weights. I take short walks to break up my day. And I love the feeling I get after running. I am a 2-mile runner, max.

- I spend time with my dog.
- I absolutely love being with my friends and laughing. I enjoy being funny. I take myself lightly. I laugh at myself.
- I spend time meditating every morning – on things that I want to improve on and am grateful for.
- I visualise a future where things go *right*.
- I send positive thoughts to everyone – even the people I don't like. This one is hard.
- I try to forgive, until I forgive. This one is harder.
- I journal in different-coloured journals: black for things that hurt me or challenges that I am processing. Blue or, better, pink for stuff that makes me happy, that I am grateful for, that I am planning, etc.
- I accept that I can't control everything.
- I feel my feelings. I acknowledge that I am not my feelings, and I am not what happened to me.
- I say, 'thank you' and I specify why. Sometimes people don't know why we are grateful. When we say it, we not only solve the mystery, but also optimise the probability that it will happen again – because it shows that we were paying attention.
- I ask for help and try to help people.
- I try to have as much fun as possible, especially around work. I actually plan fun in my life. It's a huge mood booster.
- I do work that aligns with my values and gives me a sense of life purpose.

RESOURCES

You can find more information on wellbeing, happiness practices and world happiness talks on the WOHASU app.

For more information on the work and policy of the wellbeing movement:

https://worldhappinesssummit.com/

https://wohasu.com/

https://worldwellbeingmovement.org/

Other useful links:

https://greatergood.berkeley.edu/

https://actionforhappiness.org/

https://www.habitualroots.com/uploads/1/2/1/3/121341739/whatarethebenefitsofmindfulness_1.pdf